From Canoes to Cruisers

The Maritime Heritage of Long Island

Written and Illustrated
by
Joshua Stoff

Empire State Books
Interlaken, New York
1994

All drawings by the author.

Nineteenth century engravings, pp. 35, 51, 55, 61: John W. Barber and Henry Howe, *Historical Collections of the State of New York* (New York, 1841), from a copy in the Long Island Studies Institute, Hofstra University.

Library of Congress Cataloging-in-Publication Data

Stoff, Joshua.

From Canoes to Cruisers: The Maritime Heritage of Long Island / written and illustrated by Joshua Stoff.

p.   cm.

Includes bibliographical references.

Includes index

Summary: Provides an overview of Long Island's maritime history.

1. Maritime—New York (state)—Long Island—History—Juvenile literature. I. title.

TL522.N7S86 1994   629.13'009747'21—dc20   90—47647

Manufactured in the United States

ISBN: 1–55787–110–8 (Cloth)
ISBN: 1–55787–111–6 (Paper)

A *quality* publication of
Heart of the Lakes Publishing
Interlaken, NY 14847

Dedication

For Mom

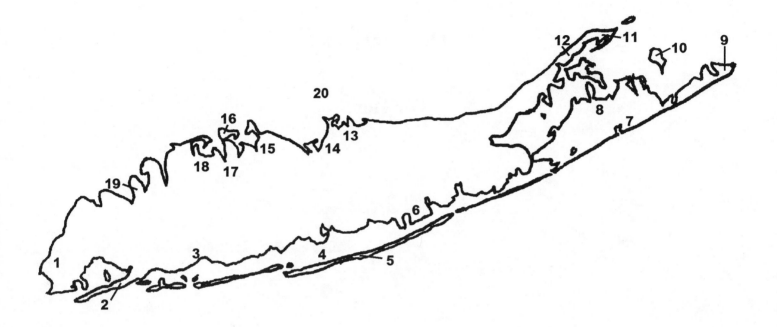

1. Brooklyn Navy Yard
2. Rockaway
3. Freeport
4. Great South Bay
5. Fire Island
6. Mastic
7. East Hampton
8. Sag Harbor
9. Montauk Point
10. Gardiners Island
11. Orient Point
12. Greenport
13. Port Jefferson
14. Setauket
15. Northport
16. Lloyds Neck
17. Cold Spring Harbor
18. Oyster Bay
19. Kings Point
20. Long Island Sound

Contents

	Foreword	7
	Introduction	9
1.	Indians on the Waters	11
2.	Dutch and English "Discover" the Island	15
3.	Shore Whaling	17
4.	Pirates!	19
5.	Early Shipping and Shipbuilding	21
6.	The British Are Coming!	23
7.	The Whaleboat Raiders	25
8.	Lighting the Way	27
9.	The Second War with England	29
10.	Whaling on the Open Seas	31
11.	The Whalers of Sag Harbor	35
12.	Whaling from Cold Spring Harbor	37
13.	Shipwrecks!	39
14.	The Lifesavers	43
15.	Shipbuilding on the North Shore	45
16.	Ships from Port Jefferson	47
17.	Fertilizer from the Sea	49
18.	The Schooner Years	53
19.	Building Warships in Brooklyn	55
20.	The *Monitor*	57
21.	The Golden Age of Steamboating	59
22.	The Baymen	63
23.	The Fishermen	67
24.	The Gold Coast Sailors	69
25.	Gyroscopes for Ships	71
26.	Port Jefferson: End of an Era	73
27.	World War I Naval Action off Long Island	75
28.	New Warships from the Island	77
29.	The Rumrunners	79
30.	Defending New York	81

31.   The "Invasion" of Long Island   83
32.   "Long Island" in Distant Waters   85
33.   U-Boats off our Shores   87
34.   Boats from a Planemaker   89
35.   Long Island Submarines   91
36.   Maritime Training on Long Island   93
37.   Searching the Seas   95
38.   The Beaches   97
39.   Long Island Waters Today   99
       Further Reading for Younger Readers   101
       Bibliography   102
       Long Island Maritime Museums and Related Sites   104
       Marine Education Centers   106
       About the Author and Illustrator   107
       Long Island Studies Institute   108
       Index   109

Foreword

I stand as on some mighty eagle's beak,
Eastward the sea absorbing, viewing, (nothing but sea and sky,)
The tossing waves, the foam, the ships in the distance,
The wild unrest, the snowy, curling caps—that inbound urge
    and urge of waves,
Seeking the shores forever.

From "Montauk Point" by Walt Whitman (1819–1891)

World-famous poet and native son, Walt Whitman celebrated the Long Island he knew so well in much of his poetry—and often his focus is on the sea. In his poem, "A Song of Joys," he vividly describes the thrills and excitement of whaling:

O the whaleman's joys! O I cruise my old cruise again!
I feel the ship's motion under me—I feel the Atlantic breezes fanning me,
I hear the cry again sent down from the mast-head—There—she blows!
Again I spring up in the rigging, to look with the rest—We see—we descend,
    wild with excitement,
I leap into the lowered boat . . .

Whaling is one exciting aspect of Long Island's maritime heritage, but throughout our history, the sea has had an important influence on the lives of all those who live on Long Island. Joshua Stoff, who wrote and illustrated the Long Island Studies Institute publication *From Airship to Spaceship: Long Island in Aviation and Spaceflight* for younger readers, has provided this companion book on our maritime heritage. Each of the chapters is accompanied by one of his own drawings of maritime scenes. There are suggestions for further reading and a bibliography. We have added a list of places to visit and resources for marine education.

Long Islanders are never more than ten miles from the ocean, bay, or Sound. It has been said that Long Island is the only place where you can "see a Sound and hear a C [Sea]," and tourist agencies proudly proclaim, "From Sound to Sea, Long Island is the Place to Be." Although in 1985 the United States Supreme Court officially declared Long Island to be a peninsula,* it is truly an island surrounded by water, as we know if we try to go off-island and must pay a toll to cross one of the many bridges at the western end or take a ferry to the Connecticut mainland from Port Jefferson or Orient Point.

Those of us who live on Long Island or are visitors to the Island have the opportunity to enjoy the water and beaches—swimming, sailing, clamming, surfing, shell collecting, and fishing. Part of our legacy from the past is the history that Mr. Stoff describes in this book, and we hope it will enable another generation to appreciate the influence of the sea on this island. Many maritime museums and

---

U.S. v. Maine et al, 469 U.S. 504; see R. Lawrence Swanson, "Is Long Island an Island?" *Long Island Historical Journal* 2 (Fall 1989): 118–27.

organizations preserve this heritage and enable us to see another dimension of the past. We, too, can experience the joys that Whitman proclaimed:

> O to have been brought up on the bays, lagoons, creeks, or along the coast!
> O to continue and be employ'd there all my life!
> O the briny and damp smell—the shore—the salt weeds exposed at low water,
> The work of fishermen—the work of the eel-fisher and clam-fisher.
> —From "A Song of Joys"

Dorothy B. Ruettgers, a member of Hofstra's adjunct faculty who taught elementary school for many years, has edited this book, and ensured it is accessible for younger readers. We also acknowledge and appreciate the comments of others who have reviewed the manuscript, including Ann Gill, Director, and Ina Katz, Curator, of the Cold Spring Harbor Whaling Museum and Judith Spinzia, co-author of *Long Island: A Guide to New York's Suffolk and Nassau Counties*. Peter Bentel provided design advice. Irene McQuillan, the Institute secretary, patiently and efficiently entered the manuscript and revisions on the computer.

Natalie A. Naylor, Director
Long Island Studies Institute
Hofstra University

Introduction

Long Island is a place with a rich maritime heritage. From the small coastal trade vessels and fishing boats of the American colonists, to the nineteenth century whaling ships, clippers, and steamships, to today's impressive freighters and supertankers, one thing is clear—ships helped build Long Island into what it is today. Maritime industries clearly encouraged Long Island's economic development. In the nineteenth century, as the amount of available land for new farms began to grow smaller, men increasingly turned to the sea to earn a living, and successful merchants eagerly looked for new investment opportunities. Shipbuilding and coastal trading grew, and whalemen brought new wealth to Long Island communities.

Since Long Island is an island, its first contact with European civilization came by way of the sea, and the Island's industry, agriculture, and economy have expanded during the last 300 years largely because of its easy access by water. A look at any map of Long Island tells us that we were, and still are, a seafaring people. To the north is the Long Island Sound, to the east is the Atlantic Ocean, to the south is the Great South Bay and the Atlantic, and to the west is New York Harbor. Every hour of every day, ships of all types sail the waters around us. There are huge cargo ships coming and going, oil tankers, commercial and sport fishing boats, and untold numbers of pleasure boats, as well as Coast Guard cutters, tugboats, and garbage barges. Without doubt, more pleasure boaters, under sail or power, are to be seen on the Long Island Sound than on any similar body of water anywhere in the world.

Long Island itself has a long narrow shape resembling a fish. Its eastern end is split by Peconic Bay with twenty-five mile and thirty-five mile peninsulas forming the North and South Forks. Most of the island is low and flat, but on the North Shore, bluffs rise to a height of 200 feet. Along the South Shore, from the western end to about thirty miles from Montauk Point, a barrier beach protects the waters of the Great South Bay from the open sea and helps to provide a fine body of water for boating and fishing. Along the entire North Shore, for over 100 miles, runs a protected waterway known as the Long Island Sound. It is essentially a back door from New York City to the sea. Dutch Captain Adriaen Block was the first in a long line of outstanding seamen who have contributed to the history of the Long Island Sound and helped to make this remarkable body of water famous.

In the eighteenth and nineteenth centuries, the life of almost every Long Islander was somehow tied to the sea, and the island itself was surrounded by a sea of ships. The waters provided food as well as efficient transportation.

Blacks and Native Americans made major contributions to the whaling industry; indeed, it was the Indians who first taught the white men how to catch whales. Since the birth of America, there have probably been more naval battles near Long Island than any other place in the country. The waters off Long Island are littered with the wrecks of warships from the Revolutionary War, the War of 1812, World War I, and World War II.

Long Island's maritime heritage is an exciting story, full of pirates and shipwrecks, whalers, warships, and sea battles.

Here then is our history . . . .

1. Indians on the Waters

The earliest inhabitants of Long Island were Indians, or Native Americans as they are also now known. They had lived here peacefully for hundreds of years before the Europeans came. To this day, names of many Long Island places reflect the Indians' presence: Massapequa, Peconic, Montauk, Manhasset, Patchogue, Connetquot, Merrick, and many others.

The Native Americans on Long Island generally lived in small villages near the sea. The huge mounds of oyster, clam, mussel, and other shells found at old Indian campgrounds indicate that the sea supplied most of their food. These people caught fish in various types of nets, as well as by harpooning them with spears or by shooting them with bows and arrows. The waters off the shores of the Island were filled with more than 200 types of fish as well as many varieties of shellfish. The Indians used small silver fish called menhaden to fertilize their fields of corn, and it was from the Indians that the settlers learned the value of these fish. Clam shells also were made into tools.

The Native Americans lived near the sea not only to get food, but also because there were various sea shells which could be made into wampum. Long Island Indians were very skilled in making beads from shells, and the beads were called wampum. Many shells were too easily broken, but the shells of the whelk and the large clams (called quahogs) were thicker and could be drilled and shaped into beads. The beads were white (if they were made from the whelk or large part of the quahog shell), or purple (if they were made from the purple area where the muscle held the two parts of the shell together). The purple beads were more valuable because there was less purple area on a quahog shell. When the Europeans came, they brought tools which made the holes in the beads easier to drill and the beads easier to shape. Beads were about 1/8 inch in diameter and 1/4 to 1/2 inch in length. Native Americans strung the beads together to make them easier to carry. Both white and purple wampum were valuable items to use in trading, especially with the inland Indians, who had no shells and were not skilled in making wampum. The wampum was sewn to clothing and made into strings or belts which were used in ceremonies, as a way of remembering events, and when treaties were being made.

In their fishing, and for traveling by water, the Indians used canoes, sometimes made from heavy elm bark, but more often hollowed out of logs ("dugout" canoes). As most of their living came from the sea, and since Long Island waters were their avenues of communication, the construction of canoes was a major occupation. Canoes were made by burning and scraping the inside of a large, fallen tree, usually pine, oak, or chestnut. A dugout could be shaped by one man in ten to twelve days using stone tools. The largest of these canoes were forty or fifty feet long and could carry up to forty men. The finished canoes were clumsy, slow, and heavy, but they served the Indians' purposes well.

As whales were often seen near the shores of Long Island, it was natural that the Indians learned to catch and use them. Long Island's first whalemen were Indians, who paddled offshore in dugout canoes, armed only with stone-tipped spears. Whales were valuable to the Native Americans as a source of meat, oil, and bone. The Indians drove the whales into shallow water and then stabbed them with their spears, weakening them by many small wounds. Often several canoes loaded with men were used in these attacks.

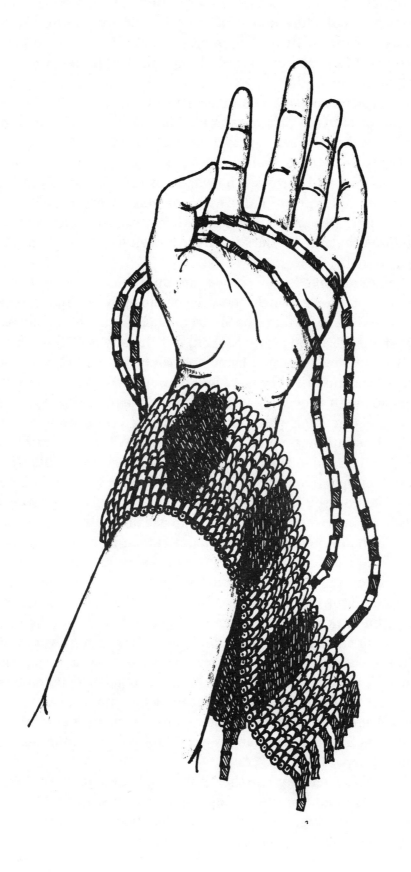

The early English settlers of Long Island were quick to realize the great importance of whaling near the shore and the great profits to be had. They eagerly sought out the local Indians and hired them to hunt whales. Friendly Indians and a favorable location are two reasons why American whaling began on Long Island. Indians served on Long Island shore whaling crews right through the seventeenth and eighteenth centuries until shore whaling declined in about 1800, and the large fleets of whaling ships began to sail from Long Island.

Indians continued to be involved with whaling as it developed into a large-scale industry in the first half of the nineteenth century. When fleets went out from Long Island ports to the whaling grounds of the world, Shinnecock and Montauk Indians were in the crews, often serving as harpooners.

2. Dutch and English "Discover" the Island

The first Europeans to sail through Long Island Sound and set foot on Long Island were Dutch explorers, led by Henry Hudson and later by Adriaen (or Adrian) Block. Henry Hudson was English, but sailed under the Dutch flag. On his 1609 voyage on the *Half Moon,* some of his crew landed on Coney Island on southwestern Long Island and were greeted by Canarsie Indians. His mate, Robert Juet, wrote in his journal of the many large fish in the waters.

Captain Block was a Dutch lawyer who had given up his law practice for a more adventurous life. In the summer of 1613, he sailed to what is now Manhattan Island on his second fur trading expedition. His ship, the *Tiger,* was anchored in the Hudson River, loaded with furs for the return trip to Amsterdam, when a fire broke out and destroyed the ship. Block and his crew set up a camp near the southern tip of Manhattan Island and began construction of a new ship, the *Onrust* or Restless. By late spring, Block was able to launch the first ship ever built in what is now New York State.

Because he was an explorer as well as a fur trader, Block wanted to explore the nearby coast. Also, the *Onrust* was not large enough to cross the ocean. Block sailed up the East River and into Long Island Sound, becoming the first white man to sail it. He set foot on Montauk Point in 1614, becoming the first European to land on eastern Long Island. He also discovered Block Island, northeast of Montauk Point, which still bears his name. (It is now part of Rhode Island.) Block was the first European to realize that Long Island was an island. After leaving Long Island, Block sailed around Cape Cod and then returned on another ship to Holland to report his discoveries. In 1614, a map, based on his explorations, gave a surprisingly accurate picture of Long Island and the Sound.

Five years later, in 1619, English Captain Thomas Dermer entered Long Island Sound at its eastern end and sailed west to Manhattan Island. Thus, at least two vessels manned by white men are known to have sailed Long Island Sound before the *Mayflower* landed at Plymouth.

By 1626, the Dutch West India Company had "purchased" Manhattan Island from the Indians, naming it New Amsterdam. Later, Dutch settlements spread to the western areas of Long Island. Eastern Long Island became the frontier for English settlers who crossed the Sound from Connecticut to establish towns there in the 1640s.

It is not surprising that these pioneers usually built their settlements near the shore, for the sea was their only means of communication with the people and civilization they had left behind. By 1675, Long Island's ports were exporting corn, fish, wheat, wood, horses, and whale oil. Only a small number of the early settlements were built inland, not only because the sea was their means of communication with the outer world, but also because it was rich in useful products. Clams and eels were found in shallow waters, and oysters could be gathered in sheltered coves. Great schools of menhaden often filled the bays, furnishing bait for fishing farther from shore. Large quantities of codfish could be caught off the coast of eastern Long Island. So the early settlers could get food, communicate, and trade by way of the nearby sea.

3. Shore Whaling

The early English settlers on eastern Long Island found a profitable trade almost at their feet—whaling. The colonists used whale blubber for greasing and protecting their metal tools and whale oil for lighting. At first the colonists could obtain blubber and oil only from the whales that had been washed ashore during storms. But before long, they learned to go out Indian-style to force whales onto the beach or to kill them offshore. In fact, in 1650, John Ogden of Southampton was granted the first whaling license in America. Whaling "companies" were formed in the communities of eastern Long Island. They were simply groups of a few men who owned small boats and tools. These companies usually hired Native Americans to man the boats, and competition for experienced Indian whalers was heavy.

Having learned whaling from the Indians, the white settlers improved their methods. Metal replaced bone harpoons, and new boats were developed which were better suited to chasing whales than canoes had been. The attack on a whale was dangerous and involved a great amount of skill and time. The small boats had to be steered to within fifteen feet of a whale to give the harpooners a chance to drive in their weapons. Once the harpoon was in, the boats were towed along by the whale, and lances with more ropes attached were thrust in. If the harpoons hit a vital spot, the hunt could soon be over, but usually it lasted for several hours. After the whale had been killed, the long process of towing it ashore began. Whales were towed in at high tide, fluke first, and pulled up on the beach as far as possible. Once the carcass was on the beach, the work of processing began. Blubber, a twelve-inch-thick layer of fat, was peeled from the entire body and cut into small strips. Then it was melted or rendered into oil by being boiled in big iron pots called try-pots, which were located on the shore. After cooling, the oil was scooped into barrels for shipping and sale. An average size whale could keep two crews of five men working for a week.

Shore whaling was also practiced in what is now Nassau County, off Rockaway and Jones Beaches. During the fall, men moved into whale watch houses along the South Shore, remaining until spring. They scanned the horizon from lookout posts. When a whale was sighted, a cry went out, and the whaleboats were launched. It is interesting to note that a Long Island man was invited to Nantucket in 1672, in order to teach the New Englanders how to catch whales.

After 1700, the whaling industry on Long Island went through several major changes. "Right" whales had been killed in such large numbers that few were seen near the shore anymore. The scarcity of right whales, and the development of much larger ships, now led to whalers going to sea for months or even years at a time, looking for "sperm" whales, and carrying their try-pot stations on board their ships. (See Chapter 11.)

The "right" whales were the best type to hunt because they produced the most oil, and so were called the "right" whale. The right whale swims slowly and was an easy whale to catch. The "sperm" whales were named after spermaceti, a milky liquid found in the head of the sperm whales. It dries into a wax which was used used to make the finest candles. Spermaceti candles were expensive because they burned steadily, giving a clear, almost smokeless light, and were odorless. Tallow candles, made from animal fat, usually were smoky and smelly. Spermaceti was used to oil precision instruments even in the twentieth century.

4. Pirates!

Because Long Island stretches 120 miles east from New York, miles of forest separated the people of the East End from those in the city. Even on the North Shore, Connecticut was only a hazy line in the distance. At the end of the seventeenth century, when piracy was at its height, Long Island played an important part because people lived so far apart. In 1699, New York Governor Lord Bellomont wrote to England, "about 30 pirates came lately into the east end of Nassau [Long] Island and have a great deal of money with them; but so cherished are they by the inhabitants that not a man of them is taken up. Several of them I hear came from Madagascar . . . I too hear that Captain Kidd dropp'd some pirates in that Island . . . Arabian Gold is in great plenty there." Bellomont felt that Long Islanders sheltered the pirates and engaged in illegal trade.

The first pirates to visit Long Island were Joseph Bradish and his crew of twenty-five, in March 1699. Bradish was originally one of the crew which had mutinied and taken control of a ship and its cargo. The ship was anchored near East Hampton for several days, during which time the pirates unloaded its cargo of gold and jewels into small boats. They then sank the ship and scattered.

By far the most famous pirate to visit Long Island was Captain William Kidd, a native of Scotland, who later became a successful merchant in New York City. In 1695, Kidd was hired by a group of wealthy Englishmen to hunt down and capture pirates in order to protect their merchant trade. In 1697, he set sail for Madagascar in a thirty-four-gun (cannon) ship, the *Adventure*. Kidd's mission was supposed to be a good method of getting rid of pirates, but it turned out to be a way for making a great amount of money by seizing pirate treasure. The mission was doomed by the fact that the crew would not be paid; instead, they would only get a share of any gold or valuables seized. If they captured nothing, they would have wasted years and probably then would turn to piracy as their only way of getting rich.

After a long time, the *Adventure* captured several North African ships and a large, richly-laden merchant ship owned by people from the Middle East, but never any pirates. The English noblemen who had sent Kidd out now considered him a pirate, and the king ordered his arrest. After his strange voyage, Kidd appeared at the eastern end of Long Island, in June 1699, in the *San Antonio*, a ship he had captured, and anchored off Gardiners Island. Kidd purchased supplies from John Gardiner (who owned the island) and gave him gold and jewels in return. Kidd then went ashore on Gardiners Island and buried most of his captured treasure, which consisted of gold bars, silver bullion, and jewels.

From there Kidd travelled to Boston to turn himself in to English authorities, hoping to be pardoned. Kidd claimed he had been forced into piracy by his mutinous crew, but the authorities did not believe him. He was hanged in England in 1701. His treasure probably was dug up and returned to England, but over the years many people have tried unsuccessfully to find it on Gardiners Island.

5. Early Shipping and Shipbuilding

Because they were surrounded by water, the scattered colonial villages depended heavily on ships for commerce, transportation, and communication. In the 1730s and 1740s, "landings" were established in the bays and harbors of the North Shore. Wood and farm produce were then carried from these places to New York City and to the ports of the Sound. As Long Island trade grew larger, many farms and villages began to develop on the North Shore of the Island. Fleets of sturdy little sailing vessels, which put into the harbors and bays and moored at the docks of the shore villages, sailed to and from New York City along the shores of Long Island.

To meet the demand for ships, many coastal communities turned to shipbuilding. East End towns such as Southold and East Hampton became shipbuilding centers; however, the best known colonial Long Island ship construction site was Oyster Bay. With its gently-sloping waterfront and well-protected harbor, Oyster Bay was a natural place for shipbuilding. By the late Colonial era, vessels built in Oyster Bay were sailing to all the major ports on the Atlantic Ocean.

It all began about 1745, when Samuel Townsend, a Jericho merchant, moved his business to Oyster Bay. Using profits from his business, Townsend had three new trading vessels built. From this first successful investment, Townsend created a large shipping business with ships and cargo sailing to the Caribbean, Central America, and Europe. With his growing fleet, he marketed Long Island's beef, pork, grain, tobacco, and lumber. He imported molasses, sugar, and rum, much of which he exchanged in New York for other goods for his local customers. Most of the town's population was employed in the construction and repair of ships and the exchange of cargoes.

Building about three ships a year, Oyster Bay craftsmen built a variety of vessels, from small open fishing boats to large two-masted schooners. Square-rigged cargo "brigs," which were larger than schooners, were built for transporting cargoes across the ocean. The difficult task of building a large ship required a wide variety of skilled Long Island craftsmen. First, lumbermen went into the woods to select and cut great trees for the ship's timbers. Then, the correct shapes were cut at the shipyard by hewers and sawyers. Shipwrights constructed the vessel at the water's edge, rib by rib and plank by plank. These carpenters used a great assortment of hand tools, such as augers, mauls, saws, hammers, and the special tool of the ship carpenter—the adze. Shipsmiths made all the iron work for the ship, including spikes, pins, rings, and other hardware. Blockmakers made the hundreds of pulleys needed for the ship's rigging. When nearly done, caulkers sealed the ship's planking with oakum to make it watertight. (Oakum was the fiber when a piece of rope was unraveled; sometimes it was tarred.) Mastmakers built the masts from the tall straight trees of the forests. Finally, riggers and sailmakers made the vast amount of rope rigging and canvas sails needed to operate the ship.

The outbreak of the American Revolution, in 1775, ended Oyster Bay's shipbuilding industry. The British stopped many of the ships from trading because they could not be sure whether the captains were loyal to the king or to the American side. After the war, a deep recession crippled many industries. Old Samuel Townsend had retired from his shipping business, and it would take a new century and new towns for Long Island's shipbuilding industry to be important again.

6. The British Are Coming!

During the Revolutionary War, there was one important battle fought on Long Island. It turned out to be an American defeat that almost became a disaster. On August 26, 1776, General George Washington arrived from Manhattan to personally take command of his army in Brooklyn. On August 27, the Battle of Long Island was fought. The British had more soldiers and weapons. Their troops had more experience and discipline, and their generals had better plans. After landing by ship at the Narrows in Brooklyn, the British moved north. In a long, hard-fought battle, they pushed the American forces back to shallow trenches on Brooklyn Heights. However, having driven back or captured the American forces, the British General, Sir William Howe, failed to follow up his victory by promptly attacking the weakened American army at Brooklyn Heights. Fortunately for the Americans, bad weather and Howe's delay allowed Washington to withdraw his army and its supplies in boats across the East River to Manhattan, saving his army and himself from being captured. Some British soldiers and their Hessian allies stayed on Long Island throughout the war. During the eight years of occupation, they sent supplies of wood and food, which they took from the people of Long Island, to the British troops stationed on Manhattan.

On October 12, the British general, trying to cut off an American retreat from Manhattan, moved his troops by ship from Long Island to Eastchester Bay in what is now the Bronx. However, Washington had already moved most of his forces to White Plains, leaving only a few troops on the northern end of Manhattan. On October 28, the British attacked at White Plains, driving the Americans northward, but they lost more men than the patriots, and went back to New York City. This ended most of the British naval action in the Sound during the Revolution.

During the winter of 1780–1781, a good part of the British fleet lay at anchor in Gardiners Bay off eastern Long Island. The British were keeping an eye on the French fleet which had been sent to aid the Americans and was now lying at anchor off Rhode Island. The British seem to have been on good terms with some of the residents of eastern Long Island. They even invited some wealthy loyalists from East Hampton to dinner parties on board the flagship, HMS *Royal Oak*.

On January 22, 1781, news came that ships of the French fleet were leaving Rhode Island and seemed to be close enough to chase and capture. The British Admiral sent three ships after them, including the 161–foot-long, 74–gun vessel, HMS *Culloden*. The HMS *Culloden* carried a crew of 650 officers and men. However, a gale-force winter storm soon struck the three vessels with all its fury. The captains knew that their only chance for survival in such a storm was to seek the open seas. Two of the three ships made it; the HMS *Culloden* did not. She ran aground on the point near Montauk that now bears her name. No lives were lost, but the ship was wrecked. The crew salvaged the guns and everything else they could before they burned it to the waterline. Part of her hull can be seen at low tide. It is to become an underwater park, specifically for use by scuba divers.

7. The Whaleboat Raiders

Although Long Island remained in British hands, the waters around the Island continued to be a battleground throughout the Revolution. The Sound became a "no-man's land," with American raiding parties in small, fast whaleboats coming across the Sound for surprise attacks to destroy or steal British property and provisions. In peacetime, these boats hunted whales, but now they were after more dangerous game—the British. These boats were about thirty feet long and could be rowed or sailed. They were light enough to be carried overland. Some of them carried a large gun in the bow. The whaleboat raiders, sailing from Connecticut, also crossed the Sound to kidnap prominent loyalists, who were later exchanged for captured patriots.

The whaleboat raids were very effective in interrupting the flow of supplies from Long Island to the British stationed in New York City. One of the first raids occurred in May 1777, when 170 men under Colonel Jonathan Meigs sailed from Connecticut and landed near Sag Harbor. There they surprised and captured a British fort. They destroyed twelve ships in the harbor, as well as supplies of hay, corn, oats, and rum. A second raid was made that August, when 500 men under General Samuel Parsons attacked the Presbyterian Church in Setauket. After a difficult three-hour battle, the rebels withdrew, having heard that British reinforcements were on the way. Another major attack on the Island came on September 5, 1779, when Benjamin Tallmadge made a surprise attack on a loyalist fort on Lloyds Neck. Tallmadge captured 500 prisoners in the raid and escaped across the Sound without losing a single man.

The most daring raid took place in 1780, when Tallmadge led eighty men in an attack on Fort St. George in Mastic. This fort controlled the British routes for getting supplies to eastern Long Island. After landing at Mount Sinai on November 21, Tallmadge moved his raiders into position to attack the fort on November 23. In order to avoid warning a sentry with an accidental shot, Tallmadge ordered his men to make a bayonet charge against the fort. The surprise was complete. Creeping up on the fort on all sides at once, the attackers broke through the stockade shouting, "Washington and Glory!" Within ten minutes the entire fort had been captured, as well as several British ships moored nearby.

Caleb Brewster of Setauket led the last whaleboat raid on December 7, 1782, when his whaleboats captured two British vessels off the Connecticut shore. Captain Brewster also had been involved in carrying messages to Connecticut for Washington's spy ring. Information about the British army and navy were carried by a spy on horseback to Setauket. When he passed Strongs Neck, he would check the clothesline of Mrs. Anna (or Nancy) Strong. She would hang her black petticoat and six white handkerchiefs in different patterns to indicate in which of six coves Brewster and his whaleboat were waiting to get the information and carry it across Long Island Sound to General Washington.

The whaleboat raids achieved their purpose; the British were never safe on Long Island. Unfortunately, sometimes the raids victimized patriots, too, and became an excuse for robbery. The British also used whaleboats and raided Connecticut towns, but more often they relied on their warships patrolling the Sound.

8. Lighting the Way

As Long Island has been on the major shipping lanes for over 300 years, a large number of lighthouses have been built to guide ships safely past its dangerous rocks and reefs. The first lighthouse in New York State was built at Montauk Point because of its important location. Montauk was one of the most dangerous areas in the trans-Atlantic trade routes. President George Washington personally signed the order for its construction in 1796. Whale oil was used for fuel for the light at Montauk until the 1860s, when it was replaced by lard-oil for a short time and then by kerosene. Today it is electrically operated. Montauk Light rises more than 160 feet above the Atlantic. At the bottom it is twenty-eight feet in diameter, with walls nine feet thick. By day, the big white tower serves as a signal post for sea traffic. At night, it flashes its beam far out to sea every ten seconds.

The first lighthouse on Fire Island was erected on its western end in 1825, because shipwrecks were so frequent along that beach. A replacement lighthouse, the beacon that stands today, was built in 1858. It rises 166 feet above the sea, beaming a flash every minute. Originally it was plain cement, but since 1891, it has been painted with broad black and white bands. By the 1900s, over 150,000 ships a year navigated safely into New York harbor using the Fire Island Light. In 1858, Fire Island's second lighthouse was constructed at its eastern end at the Shinnecock Inlet. Lighthouses also were built on Long Island's northeastern tip at Little Gull Island in 1806, and Plum Island in 1827. These lights safely guided ships in and out of Long Island Sound. A lighthouse was built on Cedar Island in 1839, in order to guide the Sag Harbor whaling fleet safely into port.

One of the most dangerous spots on the shore of Long Island Sound is Eatons Neck near Northport, where a lighthouse was built in 1798. In 1824, another stone lighthouse was built at Old Field. This was used by ships going to and from Setauket Harbor. Further examples of fine early lighthouses can be seen at Hortons Point (Southold, built in 1857), and Sands Point (built in 1809). The Lloyd Harbor Lighthouse, now known as the Huntington Harbor Lighthouse, was built in 1912 to replace an 1857 lighthouse. It is short, square, and has many interesting decorative wrought iron features. It is considered one of the prettiest on Long Island and is an early example of the use of reinforced concrete for a lighthouse. At the beginning of the nineteenth century, Long Island Sound was believed to have one of the best-illuminated coastlines in the United States. This was a result of the importance of shipping in Long Island's economy.

9. The Second War with England

The outbreak of fighting with England during the War of 1812 had serious effects on Long Island shipping. British warships blockaded the Sound and shipping lanes along the South Shore, cutting off Long Island's trade. Port Jefferson and other ports on Long Island were raided by the British. One of the most famous attacks occurred one night in 1813, when two British warships sailed right into Port Jefferson harbor and captured seven merchant ships lying at anchor. The only fort nearby, "Fort Nonsense," was in Poquott. When the British attack was discovered, the fort opened fire on the escaping ships with its single cannon. This had little effect on the warships, but it did manage to drive one aground on a sandbar. Rather than leave the ship to be captured, the British burned it to the waterline.

As in the Revolution, the eastern end of Long Island was troubled by British raids throughout the entire war. Often British warships anchored in Gardiners Bay. They took whatever food and supplies they wanted from the nearby island and were very rude to the owner, John Lion Gardiner, in the process. However, this worked against the British on one occasion. Gardiner, overhearing that an attack was to be made on nearby Sag Harbor, sent his trusted black servant with a note of warning. When more than one hundred British Marines approached the town at midnight, they were met by the local militia and driven away.

There was also some naval action in the Sound during the war. American privateers (ships hired by the American government to capture enemy ships), carrying between 40 and 100 men, sailed the region, searching for British ships and attacking wherever they met them. Sometimes a privateer would capture half a dozen British ships on a single cruise. In May 1813, there was one famous engagement, when four large American privateer schooners drove off three British warships that had sailed between Block Island and Montauk Point.

In March 1814, the American frigate USS *Essex*, commanded by Captain David Porter, was captured by the British off Chile after a successful cruise during which it had sunk many British ships. Porter and his crew were set free in a smaller boat, the USS *Essex, Jr.*, after promising never to bear arms against the British again. When stopped by another British ship off the South Shore of Long Island in July 1814, Porter and several of his crew escaped in a whaleboat. They rowed in dangerous surf through Fire Island Inlet and across Great South Bay to Babylon. The people of Babylon made him prove he was an American because they feared he was an English spy. Then the whaleboat was placed on a wagon, and Captain Porter and his crew climbed into the whaleboat. A horse pulled the wagon to the Brooklyn Navy Yard where Captain and crew were received in triumph.

The worst British loss of the war occurred on January 16, 1815, when the British warship HMS *Sylph* ran aground near Southampton in a snowstorm. The HMS *Sylph* had been active in pursuing American shipping in Long Island Sound during the war. From a crew of 121, only six sailors survived.

10. Whaling on the Open Seas

By the late eighteenth century, whales could no longer be found close to the shore, forcing whalers to pursue them on the open seas. The hunting of whales took the ships on long voyages of two or three years, and sometimes even longer, as no ship wanted to return before its hold was filled with barrels of oil and whalebone. If the trip was a success (a "greasy" voyage), the captain and officers would be very well paid. If it was a failure, the crew would receive no wages for the long voyage. They only received a share of the profits.

Whaling ships normally carried a crew of about thirty men, including many Indians and African Americans. Black seamen were a common sight on nineteenth century Long Island whaling ships. For example, Pyrrhus Concer of Southampton, who had been born a slave, was a boat-steerer on the whaling ship *Manhattan*. Whaling was the first truly integrated American industry. Members of all races usually worked together in harmony.

Living conditions on the whaling ships were bad, and the food was poor. Crewmen lived on corn meal, salted fish, potatoes, and beans. Occasionally, fresh fruits could be obtained in foreign ports of call. Sickness, accidents, and death were common because of the poor diets and lack of medical care, as well as the danger of the work.

A whaling ship weighed four or five hundred tons and was built for seaworthiness rather than speed. Firmly set in waist-high bricks on the ship's deck were two or three giant try-pots for "trying out" or melting the whales' fat (called blubber) to get the oil. Above the decks hung the sleek curved whaleboats, twenty-eight feet long, pointed at each end, and capable of great speed when rowed by four or six men. Each whaleboat was equipped with harpoons and long, deadly lances used in killing the whales. (An original one of these whaleboats may be seen at the Cold Spring Harbor Whaling Museum, and a copy of one is at the Sag Harbor Whaling Museum. Many of the tools used by whalers are to be found in each of these museums. The Huntington Militia, a reenactment group, has built a replica of a whaleboat which they use in historical events.)

When a lookout shouted, "Thar she blows," indicating that a whale had been seen, the crew lowered the whaleboats and rowed toward the whale. When they were within striking distance, the harpooners threw their spear-like weapons (called harpoons) into the whale's body. These harpoons had sharp points and barbs at the end, so that they would stick in the whale, and ropes attached to the handles so that the whale could not escape. The whales would swim as fast as possible, dive, and strike out with their flukes, trying to escape from the harpoons, and pulling the whaleboats behind them. Sometimes the small whaleboats would overturn or be crushed by the flukes, and many men were killed or drowned in this way. As the boats were pulled swiftly up and down over the huge ocean waves by the whales, this came to be known as a "Nantucket sleigh ride" because the island of Nantucket had many whaling ships, and the small boats seemed to slide over the waves like sleds in winter.

Sometimes the whale died quickly, but often the boats would be towed for almost the entire day. Finally, the whale would grow tired, and was killed with lances. Sometimes the whaleboats had to row back five miles or more to reach their ship. Then the whale was brought alongside the ship and cut into pieces.

The blubber was cut into great chunks called "horse pieces" and then cut with special mincing knives into thin slices known as "Bible leaves." These were put in

WHALEMEN
WANTED.

Experienced and Green Hands are wanted for the Ship's of the

COLD SPRING WHALING COMPANY

to sail from Cold Spring Harbor, Long Island. Apply immediately to

JOHN H. JONES, *Agent.*

Cold Spring, 6th July, 1839.

Courtesy: Cold Spring Harbor Whaling Museum Collection.

Examples of scrimshaw from the Cold Spring Harbor
Whaling Museum Collection.

the try-pots to be melted down into whale oil. After 1,000 barrels of oil had been stored in the hold of the ship, the men celebrated. They would fry their doughnuts in whatever oil was left and they would have hot, fresh doughnuts to eat.

When the whale's body had been stripped of all its blubber, the whalemen would cut into it in search of ambergris, a grayish, waxy substance sometimes found in the intestines of the sperm whale. This was used in the manufacture of expensive perfume and was found only once in a great while. It was worth more than its weight in gold.

The tough skin called cracklin' was tossed back under the pots as extra fuel. Any whale meat was usually thrown to the sharks as food, the spermaceti was saved, and the whalebone (baleen) and teeth were stored as part of the cargo to be sold. Baleen (flexible strips from the mouth of the right whale) was cut into strips to stiffen ladies' corsets, make ribs for umbrellas, be carved into decorative products, or ground up for fertilizer. The sailors used some of the teeth and baleen to carve scrimshaw and make other gifts for their wives or sweethearts. Every part of the whale which could be used was carefully saved. When the ship was full, it would return home to Long Island.

It was always a joyful day when a ship came back from its long voyage. The homecoming of a whaler was certainly a major event for the eastern Long Island towns. The whole town came down to the wharf to meet it. If the voyage had been successful, the captain and officers would take home enough money to live comfortably for a few years. After several successful voyages, they could buy a farm and retire from the dangerous job of whaling.

Wives sometimes accompanied their captain husbands on the long whaling voyages. Martha Smith Brewer Brown was a "whaling wife" who sailed on the *Lucy Ann* out of Greenport in 1847. Her husband, Captain Edwin Brown of Orient, had returned only a few months before from a thirty-month whaling trip. Mrs. Brown spent eight months in Hawaii where she gave birth to their son, William, while her husband was pursuing whales in the Northern Pacific. She was reunited with her husband on his homeward journey and the *Lucy Ann* returned to Greenport after a twenty-two-month voyage. The Browns spent the rest of their lives in the Orient. Captain Edwin became a farmer and Martha later owned and managed a boarding house for summer visitors.

Sailors, whether captains or cabin boys, loved to tell stores of their adventures at sea. Thus, we have an unusual but true story of an adventure of Captain Mercator Cooper of Southampton and his crew of the whaler *Manhattan* in 1845. The *Manhattan* was capturing whales in the Pacific Ocean and needed a fresh supply of wood and water. They discovered shipwrecked Japanese sailors whom Captain Cooper promised to take back to Japan. He was taking a chance because Japan had forbidden foreigners or their ships to enter Japanese ports. They had even fired on an American ship in 1837 when it had tried to bring other stranded sailors home.

Captain Cooper put four of the Japanese sailors ashore to tell the officials why the *Manhattan* was sailing into the port. When the ship was finally allowed to anchor, only the Japanese sailors were allowed to go ashore. Many Japanese, from important officials to ordinary people, visited the *Manhattan* during the next three days. Then the ships sailed away. Captain Cooper brought back charts of the Japanese waters which Commodore Matthew Perry used eight years later when he "opened" Japan with an agreement which allowed American and other ships to enter Japanese ports.

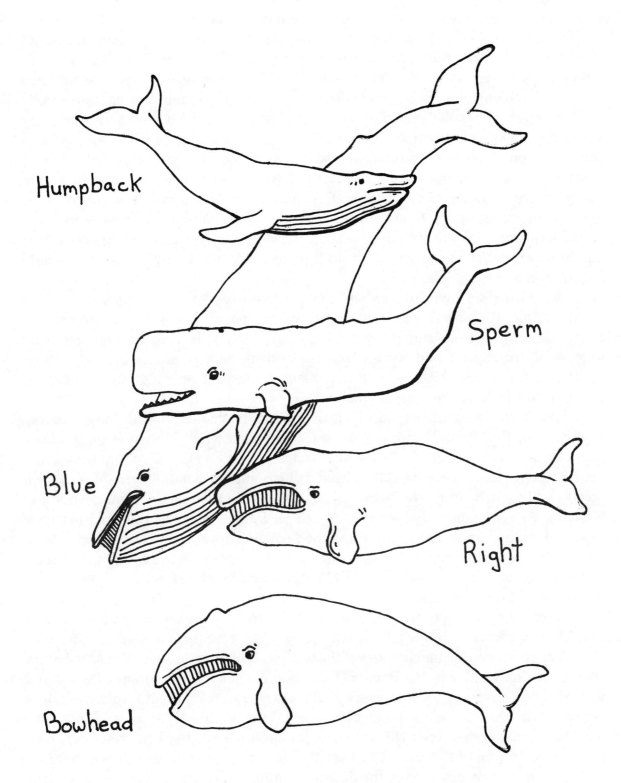

Humpback

Sperm

Blue

Right

Bowhead

11. The Whalers of Sag Harbor

Between 1720 and 1820, the whaling industry on Long Island developed through three phases: first, harvesting dead whales that drifted ashore; second, off-shore whaling with small boats (see Chapter 3, above); and third, hunting whales with large ships on lengthy trips to far off places (see also Chapters 10 and 12). Whaling enthusiasm became extremely strong in 1786, when two Sag Harbor whaling ships docked in Connecticut with more than 300 barrels of whale oil each, brought from off the coast of Brazil. However, it was not until 1817, that the first Sag Harbor whaler dared to sail around Cape Horn at the southern tip of South America.

Soon Sag Harbor, Greenport, and Cold Spring Harbor became the principal Long Island ports to become known in distant lands for their leadership in the whaling industry. Sag Harbor and Greenport built whaling ships, and they, along with Cold Spring Harbor, had great success in bringing home whale oil. The hunting of whales was a very profitable industry in the first half of the nineteenth century. This period was during the early Industrial Revolution, and the new machinery needed grease. As petroleum was not known yet, whale oil was the chief source of grease for the machinery. Whale oil was used as the fuel in lamps for lighting, too.

The greatest period of whaling lasted from 1825 to 1860. In 1836, Sag Harbor was the home port for 21 whaling vessels, and by 1847, for more than 60 whaling ships. More than 1,000 men worked on whalers, and they brought home millions of barrels of oil and pounds of bone.

The most important Sag Harbor whaling contribution occurred in July 1848, when Captain Thomas Roys sailed his whaling ship through the Bering Straits between Alaska and Russia. His became the first whaling ship to sail that far north. He also discovered a new type of whale there—the bowhead, which made whaling a profitable industry for another twenty years. Within a year, news of Roys' voyage spread, and hundreds of whaling ships headed north toward the rich Arctic waters. This large number of American whalers in the Arctic Ocean was one of the reasons the United States purchased Alaska in 1867.

Between 1800 and 1870, 125 whaling ships were outfitted in Sag Harbor. However, by 1860, the whaling boom was over. Petroleum had been discovered in Pennsylvania in 1859, so whale oil was no longer needed for grease or for lamp oil. Whaling ships also became too expensive to operate, and whales were getting harder and harder to find. The last whaling ship sailed out of Sag Harbor in 1870.

Northern view of Sag Harbor, Long Island, c. 1840

12. Whaling from Cold Spring Harbor

Between 1836 and 1862, Cold Spring Harbor became Long Island's second largest whaling port. Sag Harbor was the largest, and Jamesport, New Suffolk, and Greenport were also active whaling ports at that time. During those years nine whaling ships made forty-four voyages from Cold Spring Harbor, most of them successful. Most of the crew were Long Islanders and included Indians and African Americans. However, crew members were assembled from many places, and a good many foreign seamen also sailed on Cold Spring Harbor whalers. The supplying of provisions for the three and four year voyages provided employment for many other people in Cold Spring Harbor, such as barrel makers, sailmakers, and blacksmiths.

The Cold Spring Harbor Whaling Company was founded by local businessman John H. Jones and his brother, Walter R. Jones, who persuaded friends and relatives to join them in the purchase of a whaler. After a first successful voyage in 1837, a fleet gradually grew through the purchase of additional ships. One of their ships, the 579–ton square-rigged *Sheffield*, was the largest whaler ever to sail out of Long Island and the third largest in the entire American whaling industry.

The *Splendid*, built in Baltimore in 1832, along the lines of the great American clipper ships, was said to have been the most beautiful ship in the Cold Spring Harbor fleet. It was the experience of building the *Splendid*, combined with the advice of captains who sailed her, that contributed to the development of the American clipper ships. These were the greatest and swiftest ships on the seas during the last half of the nineteenth century.

In the 1830s, Cold Spring Harbor whalers usually sailed the Indian Ocean and the Pacific near Australia. By the 1840s, they worked in the North Pacific near Alaska. The ships often were pounded and wrecked by storms and threatened by polar ice. Cold Spring Harbor ships called at more than forty ports on five continents. The most unusual port call was a visit to Japan by the *Splendid* in 1848, at a time when that country was still closed to foreigners.

The most successful voyage by a Cold Spring Harbor whaler began in 1849, when Captain Thomas Roys sailed on the *Sheffield*. He returned in 1854, after taking 8,600 barrels of oil and 115,000 pounds of bone. While on this voyage, Roys also worked to perfect a rocket-fired whaling harpoon, which became an ancestor of the modern bazooka.

In twenty-six years of operation, Cold Spring Harbor whalers brought home more than $1.5 million worth of whale oil and bone, a great amount of money for those days. In the 1850s, however, whaling profits became smaller, and the principal owners of the whaling company had died. Without their guidance, the vessels of the whaling fleet were sold or lost to accidents. The last whaling ship left Cold Spring Harbor in 1858 and was sold four years later.

13. Shipwrecks!

Because Long Island extends east from New York City, America's busiest port, into crowded shipping lanes, it was natural for a great number of shipwrecks to have occurred on its beaches and rocks due to storms, accidents, and poor navigation. During storms there was no safe harbor on its southern coast along the entire 120–mile ocean shoreline from Montauk to Brooklyn. In fact, between 1640 and 1915, more than 600 ships sank off Fire Island alone. In one 36–month period, from 1854 to 1857, 64 ships were wrecked on Long Island shores.

The earliest recorded wreck occurred on March 8, 1657, when a Dutch ship carrying immigrants from Amsterdam went down near Rockaway. After that first sinking, a great number of vessels went down during the seventeenth and eighteenth centuries. No one even knows the names of many of these ships or what happened to their crews.

By the nineteenth century, better records were kept so Long Island shipwrecks can be more fully documented. The snowstorm of December 23–24, 1811, destroyed more lives and vessels off Long Island's North Shore than any storm before or since. Between fifty and sixty vessels went down in the Sound or were driven onto the northern shore of the Island. In most cases, entire crews died. In September 1816, a Spanish vessel came ashore a little west of Southampton. As the ship broke to pieces, streams of Spanish gold dollars poured out onto the sands. Local residents collected them for years afterward.

The *Savannah*, the first ship to use a steam engine to cross the ocean, was wrecked off Fire Island near Moriches on November 5, 1821. All hands on board, including the captain, were lost. The *Bristol*, an American ship homeward bound with many Irish immigrants, struck the shoals and sank off Far Rockaway on October 21, 1836. Again, every person aboard drowned. The *Mexico* sank in 1837. A total of 199 were lost in those two wrecks. A monument was erected in their memory in the Near Rockaway cemetery.

Another terrible tragedy occurred on January 13, 1840, when the Long Island Sound steamer *Lexington* burned and sank off Eatons Neck. The *Lexington* had been bound from New York to Stonington, Connecticut on January 13, 1840. It was advertised as "The best built vessel afloat." It had just been converted to burn coal instead of wood. This was the first trip of any steamboat using coal, and the owners were very proud of this. At about 7:00 p.m. a fire broke out, and because the boat was made of wood, the fire spread rapidly. The seas were high, and the temperature was below zero. The captain tried to reach shore, but the engines died two miles off Eatons Neck. The tiller ropes burned, making it impossible to steer the ship. The only two life boats capsized when they were launched. One hundred twenty-three people either were drowned in the icy water or were burned to death in the fire. The four men who survived floated ashore on bales of cotton from the ship's cargo.

The owner of the New York newspaper *The Sun* asked Nathanial Currier, a young man who made colored engravings, to make a picture of the disaster to be included in a special edition of his newspaper. In three days (a very short time for picture in 1840), the engraving or lithograph appeared. This was one of the very first illustrated news stories. The lithograph made Currier famous throughout the country.

Lithograph with hand-coloring, Nathaniel Currier, publisher, William Keesey Hewitt, artist. From Hofstra Museum Collection, HU 64.1 (Gift of Mrs. George M. Estabrook).

Awful Conflagration of the Steam Boat Lexington in Long Island Sound on Monday/Eve^g Jany 13th 1840, by which melancholy occurrence over 100 Persons Perished. Alternate title, *The Extra Sun.*

The freighter *John Milton* crashed on the rocks near Montauk in February 1858, after mistaking a new lighthouse on Long Island for the Montauk Light. The entire crew of thirty-three died in the gale force windsand icy waters.

The huge luxurious ocean liner *Great Eastern*, built in England and perhaps the finest ship of the nineteenth century, struck the rocks off Montauk Point on August 27, 1862, but did not sink. Fortunately, the 700–foot steamship was the first ship to have a double hull, which probably saved the 800 passengers that night. The *Great Eastern's* sister ship was not so lucky. The passenger steamer *Great Western* was completely wrecked off Fire Island near Sayville on March 26, 1876.

Accidents sometimes happened with the steamboats on the Sound. One of the worst involved the *General Slocum* on June 15, 1904. The steamer was carrying more than thirteen hundred passengers, mostly women and children, on the annual picnic of St. Mark's Evangelical Lutheran Church in lower Manhattan. A fire broke out, and the captain tried unsuccessfully to get the ship to a small island north of Long Island City. Although the ship had been redecorated just a short time before, the old life preservers had not been replaced. They were rotted and could not be used. The lifeboats could not be lowered either. One thousand and twenty-one people either drowned in the deep water or were burned to death on the ship. Investigations after the accident showed that the *Slocum* had had many collisions in the past, the crew was not well trained, and safety equipment was poorly maintained.

Ship disasters still occur off Long Island today, but the crews and passengers are usually rescued quickly by the Coast Guard or Air National Guard. The number of shipwrecks also has greatly decreased in the last fifty years due to the introduction of radar, radio compasses, and more accurate weather predictions. However, sailors must always take care in the dangerous waters off Long Island.

14. The Lifesavers

Thousands of lives have been saved from ships in distress along Long Island's shores since they were settled in the seventeenth century. At first, private citizens who lived near the shore, surfmen and baymen, would risk their lives without a moment's hesitation to help anyone in danger on the sea. They would row out in all sorts of weather to save whomever they could. If the ships broke apart and cargoes were washed ashore, the surfmen and baymen thought of them as personal gifts from the sea.

By the mid-nineteenth century, as American trade increased, the number of ships in distress and the number of lives lost grew alarmingly. Lifesaving could no longer be left to volunteer efforts. In 1849, Congress set aside money for small lifesaving huts to be built on the Long Island and Jersey shores. These simple buildings were provided with small boats and other lifesaving equipment, but they were still manned by volunteer crews. In the winter of 1850, nearly 300 lives were saved by the action of these men.

In 1878, Congress established the United States Life-Saving Service as a distinct organization, first on Long Island, and then along the entire Atlantic Coast. About thirty Life-Saving Stations were built on Long Island. These were outfitted with the most modern lifesaving equipment and staffed by professional lifesavers. Men lived year-round in the Life-Saving Stations and manned the lookout towers every day. The lifesavers' 25–foot long wooden boats were rowed by several men. It took great skill, strength, courage, and teamwork to launch a small boat through heavy surf. The Stations were also equipped with rockets and a cannon for firing ropes called lines to the ship, flares, and a breeches buoy—a round ring for survivors to step into and be hauled ashore on a rope. Every day lifesavers climbed the lookout towers, and every night they walked patrols along the beach, looking and listening for signs of ships in distress. No matter how cold or rainy the weather, the beach patrol was out every night. With their strict discipline, daily drills, and dangerous duties, the lifesavers led lives similar to those of firemen today.

Over the years of their existence, lifesavers on Long Island made several well-known rescues:

1876   *Circassian*: Mecox Station—all passengers and crew saved, but later 28 men (including 10 Shinnecocks) lost trying to salvage cargo

1882   *Margaretha*: Smith Point Station—all 22 lives saved in gale

1884   *Charlie Hickman*: Center Moriches Station—15 of the crew of 16 saved

1887   *Scotia*: Blue Point Station—nearly 1,000 passengers saved by breeches buoy

There were many more shipwrecks, and thousands of lives were saved by men of the Life-Saving Service on Long Island. In 1915, the Life-Saving Service merged with the Cutter Service to form the United States Coast Guard. Today there are only a few Coast Guard stations on Long Island, but with newer, faster boats, modern electronics, and helicopters, they each patrol a much larger area and are able to rescue people from ships in distress more quickly.

15. Shipbuilding on the North Shore

Shipbuilding became an important industry on the North Shore of Long Island during the nineteenth century. By 1840, there were shipyards in almost every coastal community. There were at least 25 shipyards in Suffolk County alone, building rowboats, small sailboats, sloops, schooners, brigs, and barks. Long Island's shape and the nearness of navigable waters made travel by sea cheaper and easier than by road. Between Long Island and New York City, cargo was carried almost totally by water. Packet sloops carrying passengers, mail, and cargo sailed back and forth along the Sound in increasing numbers. From Long Island, they carried wood, shellfish, and farm produce; to Long Island, they brought tools, clothing, and general merchandise. By 1824, one hundred vessels of all types sailed between New York and the town of Brookhaven alone.

The transportation of such products between Long Island ports, New York City, and New England was carried on by large numbers of locally built coastal trading ships. Shipbuilding carpenters built sloops and schooners from Long Island oak, chestnut, and locust trees. Northport was one of the most productive shipbuilding towns, with over 180 ships built there between 1814 and 1884. The Jesse Carll shipyard was possibly the largest on Long Island, and it built many noteworthy vessels. In addition, the harbors of Peconic Bay and Long Island Sound were ringed with shipyards which produced vessels for coastal and European trade. Cold Spring Harbor produced many ships from 1830 to 1873, and Huntington was also a major shipbuilding town from the early 1830s into the early twentieth century.

The growth of Long Island whaling caused a swift increase in the shipbuilding industry in North Shore villages such as Port Jefferson, Greenport, Stony Brook, Northport, and Setauket. Many whaling ships sailing from New England were built on Long Island. Perhaps the best-known Setauket-built whaling brig was the *Daisy*, built by Nehemiah Hand in 1872.

Robert Cushman Murphy was an ornithologist (a person who studies about birds). He wanted to learn about the birds of Antarctica, so he signed on as Assistant Navigator of the *Daisy* for the 1912–1913 whaling season to the South Atlantic. In 1936, Dr. Murphy, then with the American Museum of Natural History, offered a fully equipped whaleboat from the *Daisy* to Cold Spring Harbor if the village would build a whaling museum. That is the whaleboat you will see when you visit the Cold Spring Harbor Whaling Museum.

Although it was against the law to import slaves into the United States after 1807, some ships built on Long Island were used in the slave trade as late as the 1850s. The 100–foot-long schooner *Wanderer*, built in Setauket in 1857, was said to be the fastest ship afloat. In 1858, in Port Jefferson, the ship was refitted with extra water tanks and two cannons. It sailed to the coast of Africa, supposedly to hunt for whales. It crammed nearly 500 Africans into its hold. Five weeks later, the *Wanderer* landed the surviving 400 men in Georgia, where they were sold into slavery. The ship's real purpose of bringing Africans to be slaves was found out, and the government seized the ship. During the Civil War, the Union forces used the *Wanderer* as a gunboat. It was wrecked in 1871.

16. Ships from Port Jefferson

After the end of the War of 1812, America began to develop a much greater amount of commerce. One of the immediate effects of this on the East Coast was the great demand for new ships for trading, whaling, and carrying passengers. Port Jefferson (originally known as Drowned Meadow), with its deep harbor, nearness to cheap building materials, and closeness to the financial center of New York, became part of some of the earliest shipbuilding in the country.

As early as 1797, the first ship was built in Port Jefferson, and by the early nineteenth century, several more sloops and naval gunboats also had been built. In 1836, new wharfs, a marine railway, and an elevated road were built, allowing the central business district to grow and letting shipbuilders move closer to deep water. This made the construction of much larger ships possible. Between 1797 and 1832, only one ship a year was built in the town, but between 1832 and 1880, the average jumped to six each year. One of the main reasons the number of shipyards in Port Jefferson increased was because shipbuilding was a craft industry, taught in the shipyards through on-the-job training. The basic methods could be learned in a few seasons, and only a little money was needed to enter the business.

With the increase in shipbuilding, Port Jefferson established regular trading connections with the outside world. By the late 1830s, ships made scheduled trips between the village, New York, and New England. From the late 1700s to 1884, more than 800 boats were built in Suffolk County, and of these, 327 (or about 40%) were built in Port Jefferson. In the 1850s, with twelve shipyards in operation at once, building as many as seventeen new ships at one time, most men who lived in Port Jefferson worked in shipbuilding. The size of the ships built there gradually increased until the 1870s, when huge, three-masted schooners were built.

During this time, several historic and fascinating ships were built in Port Jefferson. The 150–ton schooner *Edward L. Frost*, built in the Bayles shipyard in 1847, had the honor of becoming the first American ship to bring cargo from Japan in 1856, after trade had been established with that country by Commodore Perry. The schooner *Henry James*, built in 1854, was part of the Union mortar fleet used in Admiral Farragut's bombardment and capture of New Orleans during the Civil War. Port Jefferson also had a famous sailmaker, Rueben Wilson. He had made the sails for the schooner *America,* which defeated an English ship in a race in 1851. This was the start of the "America's Cup" competition that continues today. Wilson moved his business to Port Jefferson after the *America* won the cup.

By the 1870s, the sailing ships and Port Jefferson shipbuilding became less important. The whaling industry was dying, and steamships were replacing sailing vessels for carrying both people and products. The Port Jefferson shipbuilders were slow to change to the construction of steamships. In 1883, a steam ferry was built for the Bridgeport and Port Jefferson Steamboat Company—a business still in operation today. A branch of the Long Island Railroad was brought to Port Jefferson in 1873. The railroad proved to be too much competition for the sailing ship, and fewer and fewer large ships were built in Port Jefferson. (See Chapter 26 for more information.)

17. Fertilizer from the Sea

In the nineteenth century Long Island had a highly specialized and important fishing industry that is almost unknown today. The Long Island Indians fertilized their fields with local fish, and the white settlers slowly adopted their methods. In the past, enormous schools of small silver fish called "menhaden" (Algonquin for "that which enriches the soil") came each year to Long Island waters where they were generally ignored because they were useless for food. However, by the end of the eighteenth century, Long Island farmlands were yielding poor crops because the soil had been overfarmed by the white settlers and was becoming less fertile.

Fortunately, in the 1790s, a pioneer agricultural experimenter, Ezra L'Hommedieu of Southold, began to promote the idea of using menhaden (now also called mossbunkers) as fertilizer for the soil as the Indians did. Within a few short years his idea took hold, and people living near the shores regularly "harvested" the bays and the Sound for fish fertilizer with which to cover their fields. It took about 15,000 fish to fertilize one acre of land, but the crops it yielded were remarkably improved. Usually the fish were plowed into the soil, but sometimes they were left on the surface to rot. In the early nineteenth century, only hundreds of thousands of menhaden were caught annually for farming, but hundreds of millions of these fish were being used by the end of the century. The mossbunker clearly played an important part in making the soil of Long Island richer. Harvests increased and farmers' profits did, too.

At first the fish were gathered only by individual fishermen, many of whom were also farmers. As demand for the fish increased, companies were formed which hired fishermen to catch mossbunkers. Most of these companies were located along Peconic Bay or the beaches of the South Shore. The fishermen used large rowboats called seine boats, pointed at both ends, with 3/4 mile-long nets stretched between them, to gather in the fish. The nets, usually full of fish, were then brought to the beach where horses pulled them in. By 1850, the first menhaden oil factory was built at Greenport, where the fish were boiled for their oil, as the whales had been. This oil was used for painting, tanning, and softening leather. The remains of the fish left after the boiling were sold to farmers to be used as fertilizer.

With the opening of the new menhaden processing factories, competition between the fishing companies led to using larger boats, usually schooners. With larger boats they could catch the fish farther off shore, using huge "purse nets." However, by 1865, factory owners decided to cut out the independent fishing companies entirely and send their own ships out to sea in search of menhaden. By 1875, the catching of menhaden was a national industry with factories from Maine to Baltimore, but Long Island was always its center. Twenty-three fish-processing factories operated here. Most were located on Barren Island in Jamaica Bay, in Sayville on the Great South Bay, and at Greenport on Peconic Bay.

PROMISED LAND
FISH PROCESSING COMPANY

After the Civil War, another change occurred in the menhaden industry as steamships gradually replaced the sailing ships for harvesting the fish. The new ships were larger and could take longer trips, but they were expensive to operate. This forced many small factories to go out of business. By 1898, the few remaining menhaden factories were sold to a large corporation, which consolidated Long Island operations on the Montauk peninsula in the section named "Promised Land." The Long Island factories were located there, not only as a business move, but also because the new summer residents and visitors to other Long Island communities strongly objected to the unpleasant smell of the fish-processing factories. Promised Land had no villages near it, and, as most of the local people worked in the plant, they did not object to the smell.

The menhaden factory at Montauk only lasted until the 1930s because natural oil (petroleum) was cheaper to process than fish oil, and other fertilizers were discovered or created. Mossbunkers still are harvested off Long Island to use as bait for larger fish.

Southern view of Greenport, 1840

18. The Schooner Years

Small, sturdy, wooden ships under sail have been a familiar sight on local waterways since the 1600s. As the population of Long Island grew through the nineteenth century, the amount of coastal traffic also grew because the new settlers needed to buy and sell various goods. A steadily growing fleet of small sloops and schooners sailed along the sheltered North Shore. (Schooners were ships with at least two masts; sloops had one.) By the 1830s, the little village of Stony Brook had one brig, eight schooners, and fifteen sloops transporting more than 4,000 cords of wood annually to New York City and New England. (A brig has two square-rigged masts.)

From Long Beach, one day in 1850, a young man wrote, "We counted within eye range from west to east 64 sailing vessels, sloops, schooners, and coasters belonging to various ports of the South Shore of Long Island, some going to, others returning from, New York and places on the Hudson. Farther out on the ocean were within sight at the same moment another 11 square-rigged ocean-going ships, some just completing their maybe long and tempestuous voyage, others outward bound."

The landings where these ships stopped were village crossroads and community centers where farmers, sailors, and businessmen could meet, exchange news, and gossip. The largest of the schooners sailing from the Island carried pine, oak, bricks, sand, clay, and gravel as far away as Central America and Africa. Port Jefferson was made an official U.S. port of entry in 1852, and in 1875, 239 ships unloaded 30,000 tons of goods there.

This coastal trade and the growth of whaling brought many shipbuilders to Long Island. Long Island had the advantage of a good supply of wood, and shipbuilders found conditions in its sheltered harbors perfect for carrying on their trade. Some of the earliest schooner and sloop building in the country took place here.

In the middle of the nineteenth century, the development of American merchant ships reached its height. The white sails of American square-rigged ships and schooners dotted every sea, and many had been built on Long Island. Long Island harbors reflected this growth. New wharves, seaside factories, and shipyards were built. Schooners went to and from Long Island ports on regular schedules to New York, New England, and ports around the nation and the world. These ships were built for speed, and their captains tried to keep to their schedules regardless of weather.

Schooners traded up and down the East Coast, carrying farm produce, wood, and oysters to the cities, and bringing back coal, molasses, and merchandise such as clothing and tools in return. One schooner is known to have sailed from East Rockaway to Spain, carrying flour ground in Rockaway and boards from Rockville Centre. Such long journeys were not unusual. The sailing captains acted as commission merchants, buying cargoes of cloth, furniture, and other supplies for Long Island stores and individuals and, in return, selling the Island's fresh produce, seafood, and wood. Long Islanders, as well as the rest of Americans, used the sea to make their products, ships, and sailors known worldwide.

HERCULES
USS OHIO
~~~~~~~
~ 1820 ~

19. Building Warships in Brooklyn

Brooklyn, at the extreme western end of Long Island, was the home of much shipbuilding and shipping activity. One of the major developments, which greatly increased Brooklyn's growth as a seaport, was the construction of the Atlantic Basin. Until 1840, the western shore of Brooklyn had many tidal flats (land above water only at low tide) and shallow ponds. In that year, Daniel Richards had the idea of dredging out and constructing a huge area in which ships could be protected from storms while they were loading or unloading their cargoes at nearby warehouses. After raising a large sum of money, Richards had the whole area dug out and the surrounding land built up. Then he built a half-mile-long row of four-story granite warehouses with a 200–foot-wide passageway through the center. This opened into a basin or rounded harbor capable of holding hundreds of large sea-going ships. Additional piers, wharves, and warehouses were built around the basin. When it was completed in 1850, Brooklyn had far better wharves for trading ships than anything New York City could offer. Dock workers could easily transfer goods from ship to storage without any expensive or time consuming transportation needed in between.

In 1801, the federal government had bought a shipyard on the Brooklyn shore from a local shipbuilder. Over the next 150 years, the government built many warships for the American fleet at what was now called the Brooklyn Navy Yard. In 1815, the frigate *Fulton* was launched, the first steam-powered warship built by any nation. The *Ohio*, launched in 1820, was an important early warship and became the flagship of the Atlantic fleet. Many foreign shipbuilders copied her design and construction, and her figurehead of Hercules may still be seen in Stony Brook today (see illustration). The Brooklyn Navy Yard has the oldest dry dock in the country, built of solid granite in 1851. In 1856, the steam frigate *Niagara* was launched at the Navy Yard. It laid the first trans-Atlantic telegraph cable in 1860. In fact, there was so much shipbuilding in Brooklyn at this time that, in 1864, the Navy Yard employed 6,000 workers. (For later years of the Brooklyn Navy Yard, see Chapter 28.)

Northern view of the Navy Yard at Brooklyn, c. 1840

20. The *Monitor*

By far the most historic vessel ever built on Long Island was the Civil War ironclad warship *Monitor* (shown in the illustration). The *Monitor* was designed and built under great pressure, because it was known that the Confederates were already building an iron-covered warship and planning to use it to attack the Union fleet which was anchored off Virginia. Swedish-American inventor John Ericsson designed the ship. He had offered the design previously to the French without success. It had an iron hull, an iron-covered deck, and was powered by a steam engine. In the middle of the 172–foot-long deck was a bold, new change in naval design. It was a revolving turret with two big cannon protected by eight inches of iron. Below the turret, the flat deck barely rose a foot above the waterline. Nicknamed a "tin can on a shingle" or "cheesebox on a raft," this was the first revolving turret ever mounted on a warship, and it greatly changed the way navies fought. Cannon could be turned and fired in more than one direction, instead of the whole ship having to be turned. The steam-powered *Monitor* could perform complicated maneuvers as it did not rely on the wind, and its iron sheathing kept the cannonballs from going through.

On January 30, 1862, the ship was launched by the Continental Iron Works in the Greenpoint section of Brooklyn. It was built in 100 days at a cost of $175,000. The name *Monitor* was chosen as a warning to wrongdoers. The ship quickly sailed to the Chesapeake Bay, where the Confederate ironclad, *Merrimack,* was ready for action. On March 8, the *Merrimack* attacked the Union fleet, easily sinking two of the wooden warships. The next morning the two ironclad warships met in the world's first battle between iron warships. Although the *Merrimack* was nearly four times larger than the *Monitor*, their 150–pound cannonballs barely dented each other's armor. The two ships fought each other for more than two hours, bouncing many shots off each other, but failing to find a weak spot. Finally, both ships withdrew. The *Monitor* had saved the rest of the Union fleet. This battle proved that an iron-covered hull could stand up against cannonballs. Naval warfare would never be the same again. It was the beginning of the end of wooden battleships.

21. The Golden Age of Steamboating

The development of the steamship in the nineteenth century completely changed the shipping and shipbuilding industry. Now ships no longer would need to depend on favorable winds for power. They carried their own engines and fuel. In 1814, just seven years after the world's first steamship sailed up the Hudson River, the steamer *Nassau* was making pleasure trips between New York City and Flushing. In 1844, the main line of the Long Island Railroad was built to Greenport, and a steamship route was established from there to Connecticut. There passengers would board another train in order to complete travel from New York to Boston.

The next step was for steamships to carry products between the eastern villages and New York. By the early 1850s, regular freight and passenger steamboat service had begun at several North Shore communities such as Lloyds Neck and Port Jefferson. The Bridgeport and Port Jefferson Steamboat Company was formed in 1883, providing regular service between Long Island and Connecticut. This is one of the oldest ferry companies in the United States and is still in service today.

From 1840 to 1915, another popular form of Sound steamer was the commuter boat, which traveled between the rapidly growing communities of Long Island's North Shore and New York City. This service was used most often by salesmen, storekeepers, and businessmen who only needed to go to New York about once a week, rather than people who made the journey every day. However, many of the prominent stockbrokers, attorneys, and other businessmen, who commuted from Roslyn, Sea Cliff, Glen Cove, Great Neck and other communities along the North Shore, preferred the slower but more relaxed atmosphere provided by the steamboats to that of the cars of the Long Island Railroad. These vessels also were more convenient because they docked directly in lower Manhattan, near the big firms of Wall Street. Because these boats did not need staterooms, they could carry far more people in a small space than the overnight steamboats going to eastern Connecticut, Rhode Island, or Boston. The steamers usually began their trip at about 5:30 or 6:00 a.m., picked up passengers or freight at several places, and docked in Manhattan well before noon. The return trip left the city at about 4:00 p.m. and reached its final destination at about 6:30 that evening. Farmers with produce to sell in New York City used the steamboats regularly. The finest steamer to run from Hempstead Harbor to Manhattan was the *Seawanhaka*, built in 1866, and sailing every morning until June 1880, when she burned and sank in the East River with the loss of forty lives.

Long Island Sound was filled with huge, luxurious steamships running between New York and Boston from the 1870s to 1930s. These trips usually took ten to twelve hours, and passengers slept overnight in staterooms. The main part of the forward deck held cargo, but the stern had a very fancy entrance hall. The passengers would enter here and then, after getting their stateroom keys, would go up wide mahogany stairs to the Main Saloon, which was often two decks high. Here there were carpets, huge sofas and chairs, and often potted palms. The staterooms were on both sides on both decks. These were small, containing only one double-decker bunk and sometimes a sink or stool. Nightboats on Long Island varied in size and furnishings according to the companies which owned them. The famous Fall River Line had the largest and fanciest of them all. Frequently in the summertime, residents of the North Shore of Long Island could watch the nightly parade of brilliantly lighted steamships on their way to Boston.

FOR
WHITESTONE, BAYLIS' DOCK.
GREAT NECK, SANDS POINT,
GLEN COVE
MOTT'S DOCK,
Glenwood & Roslyn,

THE STEAMBOAT
SEAWANHAKA!
CAPTAIN CHARLES POST,

Will, on and after MONDAY, OCTOBER 8th, 1866, leave Roslyn every morning---Sundays excepted---at 7 o'clock, Glen Wood, 7-10, Mott's Dock, 7-15, Glen Cove, 8, Sands Point, 8-22, Great Neck, 8-45, Baylis' Dock, 8-55, Whitestone, 9-05.

Returning, will leave New York from Peck Slip, Pier 24, East River, at 3-15, P. M. The Arrowsmith will discontinue her trips after the 8th.

David Hyne. Steamboat Printer, 109 Nassau St., N. Y.

Although not as large and fancy as the steamers of the Fall River Line, the steamships of the Montauk Steamboat Company provided a popular way of traveling between the East End of Long Island and New York. Various steamers served on the Sag Harbor-Greenport-Orient-New York Line as early as 1859, although the Montauk Steamboat Company was not officially formed until 1876. The ships usually traveled to New York overnight and had berths for more than one hundred passengers. Considerable competition for passengers existed at this time between the steamship company and the Long Island Railroad. In the 1880s, new 175–foot-long steamships were purchased, and for many years business was good. Eastern Long Island was becoming a popular area where wealthy New Yorkers went to spend the summer. Steamships not only carried produce and merchandise on their voyages, but now they also brought increasing numbers of vacationers as well. In the 1890s, an elegant new 238-foot-long steamship, the *Shinnecock,* was purchased. This ship was able to carry several hundred passengers at a time.

In 1899, in an effort to end competition, the Long Island Railroad purchased the Montauk Steamboat Company. But by 1915, the increasing popularity of automobiles and improved railroad service made the steamboat company unprofitable. Seeing no point in competing with itself, the Long Island Railroad ended steamboat service in 1920. The steamers sailed no more. Beginning about 1930, passengers and freight service by the steamboats on Long Island Sound began to be less used. One after another of the steamer lines were discontinued. By 1937 even the ninety-year-old Fall River Line ended, her boats scrapped. Eastern Steamship and Colonial Lines lasted a little longer, but when World War II began, the government requisitioned all their steamers for war service. Before the end of 1941 the magnificent steamers on Long Island Sound sailed no more.

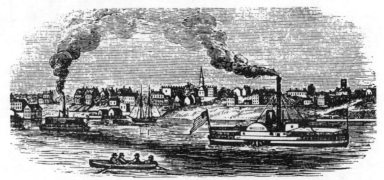

View of steamboat and Williamsburgh
(Kings County), 1840

22. The Baymen

Stretching along more than half the length of the South Shore is a broad lagoon, called the Great South Bay, enclosed by Fire Island. Various kinds of shellfish including oysters and clams find perfect conditions to live and grow in these sheltered waters. We know that the Long Island Indians harvested shellfish in great quantity for food. At the turn of the twentieth century, oystering was a multimillion dollar business on Long Island, maintaining a huge fleet of vessels and employing thousands of workers.

By the early nineteenth century, settlers along the South Shore began to harvest oysters from the Great South Bay off Blue Point. They used an open rowboat and simple, long, iron-toothed rakes (or tongs) with which to scrape (dredge) the bottom of the bay for oysters. Then a group of men appeared who depended on the products of the bay for their living. They were called baymen. The baymen used sloops which were built on Long Island. In the 1800s, during the morning the bay would be dotted with anchored rowboats and sloops, with baymen leaning over the sides gathering oysters. It was hard work, but it was a profitable business. At the end of the day the boats would head toward the wharves of the oyster factories where their catch was unloaded. In the factories the oysters were opened or shucked, the shells discarded, and the oysters put into wooden kegs. The oysters then were taken to market by the coastal trading fleet or, after 1867, by the Long Island Railroad.

In the mid-nineteenth century, a huge oyster field, stretching along most of the South Shore of Suffolk County, was harvested. Local villages prospered and the population grew. At this time, the center for gathering oysters shifted from Blue Point to Patchogue where many large oyster packing houses were built. On the North Shore, Oyster Bay was a center of oyster harvesting, but Hempstead Harbor, Huntington Harbor, and Smithtown also had oyster beds, as did bays on eastern Long Island.

In 1861, an interesting but little-known event took place in the area of the Rockaways and Coney Island. Long Island seceded from New York State! New Jersey shellfish pirates would anchor their boats off South Shore inlets, come in at night, and dig Long Island clams. After cleaning out whole clambeds, they would sail away before dawn. The clamdiggers asked local authorities and New York State Governor Morgan for protection, but no help was sent. Clamdiggers patrolled the shores nightly to protect their clambeds. They loaded their guns with bird shot, and there was shooting by both sides.

Finally, the clamdiggers notified the governor that they were seceding from New York State, but not from the Union, The clamdiggers elected Gil Davis as their governor and organized the "Rockaway Republic." Governor Morgan promptly sent the militia to arrest Mr. Davis. Davis was warned in time for him to go into hiding, and after about a week, the militia men left. Davis said, "We won our point. That militia gave those Jersey pirates such a scare that they never again bothered our clambeds."

By the 1860s, baymen were using oyster dredges. A dredge is a steel net which scrapes the oysters off the bottom. Using the dredge increased the number of oysters a bayman could get, but it also took so many oysters from the fields that not enough new ones would grow. So millions of baby oysters were "planted" or put into the bay each year in order to increase the supply. By 1890, there were twenty-five packing houses along the South Shore, with principal shipping points at Bay Shore, Oakdale,

The Clam Fleet

Clammers Homes

Schooner Buying Clams

Clammers

Treading Clams

A Chowder

Harper's Weekly, September 8, 1877

Clamming in Great South Bay, Long Island

Sayville, and Patchogue. Between sixty and seventy thousand barrels of oysters were shipped from these villages every year. Jacob Ockers of Blue Point, known as "the Oyster King," shipped 30,000 oysters to Europe annually during the 1890s. In fact, oysters were so common that the streets of Sayville were paved with oyster shells. Harvesting of too many oysters continued, however, and fewer could be found each year.

Exporting oysters to Europe stopped when World War I began. The single greatest change, however, was caused by the 1938 hurricane. That storm left the ocean with a new way into the Great South Bay through the Moriches Inlet. This increased the amount of salt in the water of the bay, causing the oysters to die. It greatly increased the population of clams, which now replaced oysters as a major crop.

Clams have been found in great numbers on the beaches and in shallow waters of Long Island, Shelter Island, Gardiners Island, the surrounding bays, and the Atlantic Ocean. Eaten raw or cooked, littlenecks, cherry stones, and quahogs have been enjoyed for centuries by Long Islanders. Quahogs were also useful in the making of wampum, an important activity among the Indians (see Chapter 1).

Clamming was not as profitable as oystering for many years because oysters were thought to be a more fashionable food. But Long Islanders continued to tread, dig, rake, or dredge clams for their own use and to sell. Many were sold to New York City markets for chowder or to eat steamed, fried, raw "on the half shell." Clambakes became a popular form of entertainment as more people came to the shore to spend their summers.

Doxsee is a name very well-known to people who buy canned clams. The Doxsee family has been clamming since the mid-1800s. At first they caught clams from Great South Bay and, when the clams became fewer, they began surf or ocean clamming. There are still Doxsees dredging clams off Jones Beach, Long Beach, and the Rockaways. Their processing plant is located in Point Lookout.

Frank M. Flower & Sons Co., in Bayville and Oyster Bay, traces its history back to William A. Flower, a bayman who lived in Mill Neck on the North Shore and began working the oyster beds in the 1850s. By the early 1900s, his grandson, Frank Flower, was harvesting clams as well as oysters, using gasoline-powered boats with dredges. When the supply of shellfish declined in the 1950s, following storms and overharvesting, Allen, Butler, and Roswell Flower began a hatchery in 1963 to raise oyster seeds. The seed oysters are taken from their Bayville greenhouse, planted in leased oyster beds in the bay, and harvested when mature. Today the Flower Company operates Long Island's only commercial shellfish hatchery.

After the hurricane of 1938, the oysters became fewer and the number of clams in the bays increased. Many baymen, who had been oystermen, became clammers. Today, there are still about fifty vessels harvesting oysters, scallops and clams off Long Island, so the tradition of the baymen continues. Scallops are a shellfish which have become increasingly important at the eastern end of Long Island in recent years. The small Peconic Bay scallops are well-known for their delicate flavor.

Pollution has affected the shellfish industry, however. From time to time, and in various places, some beds have not been able to be harvested. Over-harvesting and pollution have made it difficult for baymen to make a living from the sea. Some have had to look for other jobs, but others continue the hard life of the bayman as their families have done for many years.

23. The Fishermen

Long Island lies at the southern edge of the great fishing grounds of the North Atlantic. Without seafood, many of the early settlers on Long Island could not have survived. They were dependent on the sea, and every man had to be both fisherman and farmer. Cod, bass, tuna, bluefish, weakfish, mackerel, and flounder were caught in the early nineteenth century. Using long nets, fishermen would row around a school of fish near the shore, and then they would haul the net up on the beach. They could easily catch as many as thirty thousand fish at once in this way.

In the 1880s, Greenport alone had twenty boats that fished the waters off Long Island for bluefish in the summer and cod in the winter. Usually three men were aboard each boat, and, if luck was good, they might catch five to six thousand fish in each trip. In addition, in the shallow tidewater creeks that empty into Moriches Bay and Great South Bay, the business of catching crabs grew. The sale of bass, cod, flounder, eels, mackerel, perch, crabs, and lobsters has been an important part of the local economy for many years. The number of fishermen has increased since the 1860s, and the quality of their vessels has improved, but the fishing industry has consisted mostly of independent men using only a small crew.

Freeport was another major fishing center and from there ships were sailed by men who concentrated either on fishing in the bay or who ventured out into the deep seas. Both nets and handlines were used, and the catch generally was sold either at the dock or shipped to New York City. In 1901, Freeport shipped almost a million pounds of fish to market. On eastern Long Island, fishermen often fished in the Northern Atlantic during spring and summer, and in southern waters during the winter. Some fishermen lived in simple frame shacks, while others lived aboard their boats during the season. Only those who loved the sea in spite of the hard work involved would choose to fish for a living.

Throughout Long Island, a number of small boatyards produced the boats needed for the fishing trade. Special skiffs, built along the South Shore, were particularly suited for use on the Great South Bay. In Roslyn, on the North Shore, Thomas Clapham, a builder and designer, played an important role in the development of shallow-water vessels. During the late 1800s, he produced the Roslyn yawl, which was noted for being extremely stable. By the 1890s, fishing steamers began their work. They carried large "purse" nets which were arranged so there was no chance for a school of fish to escape once they were surrounded. These new steamers could cruise a long distance from shore where a greater number of fish was found. They began the modern fishing that still goes on by commercial and recreational fishermen from such ports as Sheepshead Bay, Freeport, Captree, and Montauk.

24. The Gold Coast Sailors

The North Shore of Long Island has many protected bays and fair winds and is ideally suited for pleasure and sport sailing. Although sailing was a great leisure activity, the dozens of yacht clubs organized on Long Island in the late nineteenth century began competition races. The yacht clubs furthered the development of small yachts and racing boats and initiated a series of national races in the late 1800s. Yachting became a major activity of the new, wealthy residents along Long Island's "Gold Coast"—on both the North Shore (of Nassau County and western Suffolk) and the South Shore (in the Islip area). Many famous wealthy families participated in yacht races. Among them were the Vanderbilts, Belmonts, and Goulds.

Long Island also launched the very first boat racing class in the United States, when a new, small, swift vessel, called a cat-boat, was converted for the Seawanhaka Corinthian Yacht Club of Oyster Bay. In 1911, the Star Class was launched. Star Class racers were small, fast sailboats that were very popular because they handled easily and were delicately balanced. Thousands were built. They are still well known in racing today. Other new, larger classes of racing boats followed, many of which were designed and built on Long Island. A good example of these are the "J" class racing yachts which were built in Greenport and once dominated the famous America's Cup Races.

Millionaire sportsmen even raced steamships, which must have seemed foolish to those who worked to earn their living from the sea. William K. Vanderbilt, Jr. and Howard Gould once arranged a series of races between their steam yachts on Long Island Sound. On at least one occasion, in 1906, local newspapers reported that the millionaires had bet $5,000 on the outcome of a race. That was a small fortune by the standards of those times. The amount of money involved in such a sport was clearly shown in a 1907 newspaper article. "Steam yachting is a sport only for men of millions. None but the wealthy can hope to own the floating palaces beside whose immense cost the finest of automobiles is in comparison as cheap as a bicycle."

25. Gyroscopes for Ships

Some of the most important navigational instruments ever built for ships were made by the Sperry Gyroscope Corporation of Brooklyn. A typical gyroscope is a very heavy, spinning wheel mounted in rings so that only one point, its center of gravity, is fixed. It is free to turn in any direction around this point. The wheel spins on an axis in much the same way as a bicycle wheel turns on an axle. Once set spinning at extremely high speeds, the gyroscope wheel keeps pointing in the same direction no matter which way you turn the mounting rings or the case they are in. Professor W. R. Johnson invented the gyroscope in 1832.

Inventor Elmer Sperry first became interested in gyroscopes in the 1890s. After a rough trip across the Atlantic Ocean, he started thinking about a direct action gyro-stabilizer to keep ships from rolling from side to side in high seas. The axis of the wheel in a stabilizer is vertical so that it senses up and down and side to side movements. The gyro-stabilizer then works to make up for this and prevent the pitching and rolling. After experimenting for a while, he interested the Navy in the invention, and they gave him an order to mount one on a destroyer in 1914. This was the first of forty-four large ships to be equipped with the Sperry Gyro-stabilizer. However, these stabilizers were so heavy and expensive that they were never accepted in general use. Nonetheless, Sperry continued to experiment with gyroscopes.

Another use of the gyroscope, which began to attract Sperry's interest about 1908, was for a ship's compass. There was an urgent need for a compass which would not react to the large amounts of steel on battleships. Sperry developed the Gyro-compass, which points to true north and is widely used on merchant and naval vessels. It is considered one of the most important navigational aids, as it is not affected by such things as the metal of the ship or electrical disturbances. By 1911, the first Sperry Gyro-compass was installed on a Navy destroyer. After the first tests were successful, Sperry received so many orders for Gyro-compasses that he had to build a new plant near the Brooklyn Navy Yard. By World War I, Sperry Gyro-compasses had been placed on most American battleships, cruisers, and submarines, and the demand for more was enormous.

After World War I, the Gyro-compass was arranged to control the ship's steering so as to hold the ship on any set course. This "Gyro-pilot" was first installed on a merchant ship in 1922, and was nicknamed "Metal Mike." For many years the Sperry Gyro-compasses and Gyro-pilots were standard on almost all merchant ships around the world. In its present, highly developed form, the Gyro-pilot, using the Gyro-compass to point to the true north, contributes to operating the ships in the best way: it steers the straightest courses, reduces wear on the steering gear, and lets the helmsman be free for other duties on the bridge.

Sperry moved to Lake Success in 1942 where it continued its operations. It became part of Unisys Corporation in 1986 and today is involved with navigation systems for submarines and other navel vessels.

26. Port Jefferson: End of an Era

The shipyards showed how life on Long Island was changing. Toward the end of the nineteenth century, whaling ships were no longer needed, and the steamer was replacing the sailing ship for fishing and trade. Occasionally Long Island shipyards built steamships, but more often their work was limited to repairing ships. In spite of changes in fishing and farming, shipbuilding did not cease. Toward the end of the century, summer visitors enjoyed the shores of Long Island, and the demand for pleasure boats grew steadily.

By 1900, only three major shipyards were left in Port Jefferson. They built both commercial and noncommercial craft: yawls, steam yachts, oyster dredges, and ferries. In 1898, a new large steam ferry, the *Park City*, was built for the Port Jefferson Ferry Company. The last large Port Jefferson-built sailing ship was the huge schooner *Martha Wallace,* built in 1901. At 1,100 tons and over 200–feet long, she was the largest sailing ship ever built on Long Island. In 1906, a secret submarine, the *Lake,* was built in Port Jefferson for the U.S. Navy. When it was tested in the harbor in 1907, however, the ship was found to be unsuitable for naval use.

Between 1884 and 1917, thirty-seven vessels were built in the Bayles shipyard in Port Jefferson. Most of these were pleasure craft, powered by wind, steam, or gasoline. One elaborate ship was the 129–ton yacht, the *Zoroya*, built in 1901. At 184–feet long, she was a magnificent ship made of the finest wood and brass.

When the United States entered World War I in 1917, America's desperate need for ships caused the shipyards on the Port Jefferson waterfront to be used again. The federal government paid to remodel the shipyards for the construction of steel-hulled vessels. Between 1917 and 1919, the number of shipyard workers grew from 250 to over 1,100, and dozens of new ships were built. In 1919, two steel-hulled, ocean-going tugboats, and two large 5,000–ton freighters were built. These were the largest freighters built in Suffolk County.

The end of World War I brought shipbuilding to an end in Port Jefferson. All government contracts were canceled, and the money spent on luxury boats began to be spent in other regions. Furthermore, the major government alterations to the shipyards had blocked any return to yacht construction as an industry. All the old equipment and buildings had been destroyed or changed in such a way that they could no longer be used for the building of pleasure boats. Shipbuilding had no future in the village. But, even if you visit Port Jefferson today, the waterfront is still full of activity, and you can imagine giant sailing ships being built for journeys to far-off places.

27. World War I Naval Action off Long Island

During World War I, German submarines were hiding in the waters around Long Island. Several merchant ships were sunk off the South Shore and Montauk Point, and the only American warship sunk during the war also went down off Long Island.

The cruiser USS *San Diego* was a heavily armed and armored warship more than 500-feet long. Between 1914 and 1917, she was the flagship of the Pacific Fleet, and in 1917 and 1918, she escorted convoys across the Atlantic without mishap. On July 19, 1918, bound from Portsmouth to New York, a huge explosion, followed by two smaller explosions, tore a hole in her side. The horrors of warfare had come to Long Island. In an unsuccessful effort to save his ship, the captain headed it toward Fire Island, hoping to run it aground before it sank. He never made it; the ship sank in 28 minutes. Most of the survivors were picked up by nearby ships, but several lifeboats were rowed ashore at Fire Island. Fortunately, only six lives were lost in the sinking. No one is certain whether it was a German torpedo or a mine that sank the ship.

The *San Diego* still rests in the waters off Long Island, 110 feet down and 9 miles southeast of the Fire Island Inlet. It is a popular, but dangerous, diving spot for people interested in exploring sunken ships.

On January 1, 1919, only a few months after the sinking of the *San Diego*, the troopship USS *Northern Pacific,* carrying 1,671 wounded American soldiers, ran aground off Fire Island. The next day was extremely stormy. In spite of the weather, several Coast Guard crews fought through the churning surf with their lifeboats and rescued all the wounded soldiers and nurses. It was a remarkable feat of lifesaving.

28. New Warships from the Island

Building warships in the Brooklyn Navy Yard has been part of Long Island's heritage throughout most of the nineteenth and twentieth centuries. (See Chapter 19 in this book.) Such ships included the battleships USS *Maine* and USS *New York*.

The *Maine* (launched in 1890) sank in Havana Harbor, in Cuba, on February 15, 1898, because of an explosion in which 260 American lives were lost. The explosion was blamed on a submarine mine, but the actual cause has never been proved. The cry, "Remember the *Maine*," caused many people to favor war with Spain, since Cuba was a Spanish colony at that time. This sinking of the *Maine* was one of the causes of the Spanish-American War.

The *New York,* launched in 1912, was the flagship of the American fleet that received the surrender of the German fleet at the end of World War I. The super-battleship USS *Arizona* was launched in Brooklyn, in June 1915, and was sunk at Pearl Harbor. The *Arizona* was the most tragic victim of the Pearl Harbor attack. At 8 a.m., on December 7, 1941, a Japanese bomb struck the forward ammunition storage area, causing the ship to blow up and sink in seconds. Today she still lies on the bottom at Pearl Harbor in Hawaii, with the remains of more than 1,000 sailors still within her hull, and is the site of the Pearl Harbor Memorial.

Between 1915 and 1945, seventeen warships were built at the Brooklyn Navy Yard, including three battleships and five aircraft carriers. In addition, hundreds of damaged ships were repaired there. The battleship USS *Missouri* was launched in Brooklyn in January 1944. In 1945, the Japanese surrender was signed on her deck in Tokyo Bay.

The Brooklyn Navy Yard was the first in the nation to receive the Navy's "E" award for excellence in production in World War II. It won that award every year until the war ended in 1945. At the height of its activity in World War II, it consisted of 270 buildings connected by nineteen miles of paved roads, more than thirty miles of railroad track, six dry docks, two piers, two enormous ship construction areas, warehouses, and lumber yards. It had a workforce of 71,000 people, and many jobs were lost when it was closed in 1966. The Brooklyn Navy Yard had been the largest industrial complex in New York State. Today, no more large ships are built on Long Island.

29. The Rumrunners

In 1919, the United States Constitution was changed to stop the sale of all alcoholic beverages in the country. There was no way such a ban could succeed. All it did was stop the public selling and drinking of alcohol and create a very profitable business for those who smuggled alcohol into the country.

Fire Island became a major hideout for liquor smugglers, who were known as bootleggers or rumrunners. Fire Island was long and mostly deserted. The bootleggers could take their small boats through Fire Island Inlet from any area on the South Shore. A fleet of old freighters was waiting in international waters twelve miles off Fire Island. Small fast boats would run out from Long Island, pick up cases of liquor from the fleet, and scoot back to safety on the Island. Even the baymen, who were skilled in the ways of the ocean, now turned to the less respectable, but more profitable, job of smuggling liquor from the freighters to thirsty Americans. Their boats, which were often equipped with surplus 400–horsepower Liberty aircraft engines, could easily outrun any boats the federal authorities used. Sailing without lights at night, they went in and out of small inlets without being caught. Upon reaching Long Island, their liquor was usually sold to local dealers or smuggled into New York City.

The Coast Guard was not used against the rumrunners until 1924, so only a small group of federal agents, with a few old Navy boats, was available to try to stop the great number of small-boat captains who found trips to the liquor fleet so profitable. The rumrunners' boats were very fast, piloted by skilled captains with a great knowledge of the local waters. Matters were complicated by the fact that Long Island officials, and even Coast Guard seamen, were bribed by the rumrunners to "look the other way" when the liquor was being smuggled in. However, sometimes the federal agents were successful. Once, in July 1922, three large ships carrying rum were captured in the waters off Long Island in one day.

In Nassau County, the inlets and bays along the North and South Shores made natural centers for illegal smuggling. In Suffolk County, Greenport and East Hampton also were major smuggling centers. Rumrunning became a way of life for some Long Islanders in the 1920s.

By 1932, the price of illegal liquor had dropped because so much was coming into the country. In 1933, the Twenty-first Amendment to the Constitution repealed the Prohibition Amendment, and selling and drinking alcohol was legal again.

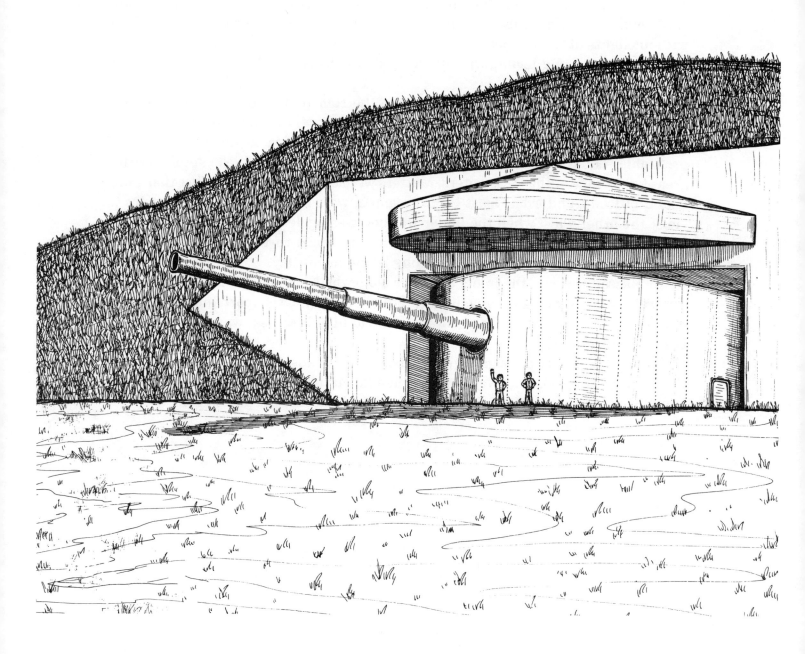

30. Defending New York

For one hundred and fifty years, one of the major reasons which discouraged any naval attack on the United States, New York, and Long Island in particular, was the building of military fortifications containing mounted guns to defend cities and naval bases at or near the sea. In fact, the construction of such forts came to be the army's major occupation between wars.

The first coastal fortifications to protect New York City were built on Long Island in the nineteenth century and were Fort Hamilton in Brooklyn (1825) and Fort Totten at Willets Point in Queens (1850). By the late nineteenth century, advances in military technology changed the emphasis from the fortifications to the weapons which protected them. The new concrete gun emplacements, although huge (over twenty feet thick) and expensive, were quite simple in shape. This was in contrast to the high stone forts of earlier times. The new fortifications were designed to blend in with their surroundings.

These forts had huge "disappearing" cannons that fired twelve inch shells. The shells weighed a thousand pounds and could travel over eight miles. They were more accurate and powerful than the guns of any attacking battleship. These cleverly made guns were designed to "disappear." A heavy weight would swing their barrels over the fort's wall where they would quickly fire, with the recoil force lowering them again. In that way they were hidden from the enemy except for the two seconds during which they were firing.

Between 1898 and 1905, several new fortifications using these guns were built. Fort Tilden, in Far Rockaway, guarded the entrance to the Verrazano Narrows. Fort Terry, on Plum Island off Orient Point, established in 1898, was the largest of the Long Island "shield" forts. A tiny island, Great Gull near Orient Point, was also heavily fortified. Rising only fifteen feet above the sea, Great Gull Island became Fort Michie in 1896, the smallest of the Long Island forts. Being stationed there must have been very hard because of the loneliness, terrible weather in winter, constant wind, and lack of fresh water. At the entrance to Long Island Sound, part of Fishers Island became Fort Wright in 1898. A total of 100 buildings were erected at Fort Wright, and more than 800 men were stationed there.

During World Wars I and II, some of the most powerful guns then in existence were placed on small islands off eastern Long Island and on Long Island itself. At the beginning of World War II, a massive fort at Montauk Point, Fort Hero, was constructed. This fort used new, long range cannons that could fire a shell weighing 2,000 pounds almost thirty miles. At the time, they were the most powerful guns in the world. The guns were placed in small, man-made hills, covered by thirteen feet of concrete and twenty feet of earth. (See illustration.) In addition, six inches of armor covered the opening, completely protecting each gun from attack from the air. Fort Hero guarded the entrance to Long Island Sound as well as southern Long Island. Big as it was, Fort Hero was invisible from the sea. All its buildings near the coast were disguised to look like a quiet Long Island fishing village.

These fortifications became a vital shield which protected several major American cities No enemy navy dared attack Long Island or New York during the Spanish-American War, World War I, or World War II.

31. The "Invasion" of Long Island

Throughout World War II, Coast Guardsmen patrolled Long Island's South Shore, looking for signs of torpedoed ships and signs of possible enemy activity. Shortly after midnight, on June 13, 1942, Coast Guard Seaman John C. Cullen left the Amagansett Lifeboat Station in a thick fog and began walking his patrol area along the shore. He was unarmed and had only gone a short distance when he noticed three men on the beach. The men claimed that they were fishermen and that their boat had run aground, but they looked and talked strangely and did not have any identification. Soon another man appeared, dragging a large canvas bag.

The men refused to go with Cullen to the Coast Guard Station and tried to bribe him not to report them. Pretending to accept the bribe, Cullen ran back to report the strange incident. Within an hour, Coast Guardsmen returned to search the beach where they soon found German uniforms, cigarettes, and crates of explosives. Nazi saboteurs had landed on Long Island only 100 miles from New York City. One of the most extensive spy hunts in American history began.

The four men were Nazi agents who had been landed by a German submarine or U-boat, U-202, just off Amagansett. They were on a daring mission to blow up American power plants, factories, bridges, and railroad terminals. By the time military officials and the Federal Bureau of Investigation (FBI) had realized what had happened, the four agents had taken the 6:30 a.m. Long Island Railroad train from Amagansett to New York City and checked into two different hotels.

Fortunately for America, the leader of the group became nervous about the plot and surrendered in Washington, D.C., a week later. He reported the others, including four who had landed in Florida. They all were quickly rounded up, tried, and six were executed. The two who cooperated with the government by testifying against the others were sent to prison and returned to Germany in 1948. Long Islander Cullen received the Legion of Merit, a military decoration given for exceptional conduct in performing outstanding service. We will never know what would have happened if the spies had not been caught so soon. This was the most spectacular war story to take place on Long Island during World War II.

A more welcome "invasion" was that of the thousands of sailors who came to the naval station at Lido Beach to be discharged after the war ended in 1945.

32. "Long Island" in Distant Waters

Although no actual combat occurred on Long Island during World War II, the name "Long Island" did see combat overseas. An aircraft carrier named after our island, the USS *Long Island,* was the first small (escort) aircraft carrier built during World War II. It was developed to provide air protection against German submarines for cargo and troop convoys all the way across the Atlantic Ocean. This was because, in 1941 and 1942, the Germans sank many Allied ships that had no aircraft protecting them.

The USS *Long Island*, identified as CVE-1, was the first of the "baby flat-tops" built during World War II. The *Long Island* started its life as a cargo ship in 1939, but in 1941, the Navy converted her for use as an aircraft carrier. The first fighters to fly off her tiny 360–foot long flight deck were Brewster Buffalos, which were also built on Long Island by the Brewster aircraft company. The *Long Island* was able to carry up to 30 planes at a time.

Tests conducted on the *Long Island* in 1941, proved the usefulness of operating aircraft off converted cargo ships. Early in 1942, pilots trained on her and then would be assigned to other escort carriers. In June 1942, the *Long Island* provided air cover for Admiral Nimitz's task force of battleships at the Battle of Midway.

The ship's most important mission was during the Battle of Guadalcanal, on August 20, 1942. American forces attacked and gained a foothold on the Japanese-held island, but they badly needed air support. Fortunately, the *Long Island* arrived and launched two squadrons of fighters and bombers directly off her deck and into battle. These planes helped win the battle for the United States.

For the rest of World War II, the carrier ferried planes to combat areas and trained pilots for carrier operations. She was retired from the Navy in 1947, but survived as a freighter until 1970, when she was scrapped. Naval history will always record how the brave little *Long Island* went to war.

33. U-boats off our Shores

Once the United States entered World War II, in December 1941, German U-boats felt free to attack shipping off American shores, especially in the early months of the war. (A U-boat is a submarine. The word comes from the German *Unterseeboot* or under sea boat.) In 1942, German submarines were particularly active all along the East Coast of the United States. The frightening war in the Atlantic was very evident along the beaches on Long Island. Life preservers and life rafts washed ashore along with the heavy oil from torpedoed ships. Many ships were sunk just off our shores. In an effort to stop this sinking of ships, the Picket Patrol was started. Groups of volunteers took specially equipped sailing yachts out of Greenport in search of German submarines and survivors of torpedoed ships.

In spite of this, many ships went down within sight of Long Island. On January 15, 1942, a torpedo fired from the U-123 hit the tanker *Coimbra* amidship, causing her fuel oil cargo to explode in flames. Only six of the crew of forty survived the sinking, which occurred only 25 miles off Quogue. Later, in January 1942, the tanker *Norness* was sunk 60 miles off Montauk; in February the tanker *Resor* was sunk by the U-578 off of Fire Island, and only two of fifty seamen on board survived. In March, the freighter *Tolten* went down off the Debs Inlet (East Rockaway), and only one of twenty-eight men survived. In April, the freighter *Arundo* was sunk by the U-136 near the East Rockaway Inlet. A British warship, the HMS *Pentland,* was sunk in September, and even as late as January 1944, the USS *Turner,* an American destroyer, was sunk off the Debs Inlet. And there were more. However, by 1943, improved anti-submarine patrols by planes and ships, and a decrease in the number of U-boats, brought greater safety to Long Island waters.

One German submarine was sunk quite close to Long Island. The submarine U-853 arrived in the eastern Long Island Sound on May 5, 1945. On the very next day she gave away her position by sinking a large freighter coming out of Rhode Island. This quickly alerted all American military forces in the area. They were only too happy to come hunt for a German submarine, as the war was about to end, and most had never seen combat. Soon destroyers, frigates, airplanes, and even blimps were searching the sea off eastern Long Island looking for the submarine. People watched the search from Montauk Point as if they were watching a circus. Soon the American ships found the German submarine lying quietly on the bottom, and they fired depth charges at her throughout the night. By the next day, floating debris indicated that the U-853 was no more. All of her crew were killed, just one day before Germany surrendered. The war was over. The last warship had been sunk in the waters off Long Island.

34. Boats from a Planemaker

As World War II was coming to an end, the Grumman Aircraft Company of Bethpage began to look for civilian products to make because they knew the government would make major cutbacks in aircraft production. They also wanted to develop a product that would use their knowledge and machinery which previously had been used for building riveted aluminum aircraft. Seeing a possible market for aluminum canoes, Grumman decided to put their idle machinery to use building them.

Grumman canoes were better than the old wooden ones as they were stronger and lighter, wouldn't crack, and had watertight compartments so they could never sink. The canoes were an instant success. Grumman built 94 canoes in 1945, and more than 10,000 in 1946. In the 1950s, Grumman canoe production was moved to upstate New York. Grumman's Metal Boats Division prospered through the 1940s and 1950s. Soon they added a fifteen-foot-long aluminum fishing boat, a nineteen-foot-long runabout motorboat, and a small nine-foot-long aluminum sailboat. Grumman boats were the only mass-produced boats designed and built on Long Island. However, Grumman no longer builds canoes.

In the 1950s, there was much interest by the government in a new type of ship, the hydrofoil. A hydrofoil is a boat that, as it accelerates to high speed, rises on the lift of what can only be described as wings running through the sea. At full speed, the hull (body) is lifted completely above the water, eliminating the heavy drag of a submerged hull and making much higher speeds possible. In 1957, the government gave Grumman the first contract to build a large hydrofoil. Work began on the craft at Bethpage in 1960, and it was launched on Long Island Sound in 1962.

Grumman's experimental H. S. (Hydrofoil Ship) *Denison* was the world's first high-speed, ocean-going hydrofoil. At 129–feet long, the sleek vessel was lifted out of the water at high speed by three sets of foils or wings, arranged rather like the landing gear of an airplane. At full speed, the 14,000 horsepower engine drove the ship along at sixty knots or sixty-nine miles per hour. This is extremely fast for a ship. The *Denison* once went from Oyster Bay to Newport, Rhode Island, in just two hours—a record for any type of ship.

Based upon its experience with the *Denison*, Grumman designed and built the *Dolphin*, an eighty-passenger hydrofoil ferry in 1966. After being successfully tested at sea, the vessel was shipped to a Spanish firm, where it was put into service as a ferry in the Canary Islands, off the coast of West Africa. Grumman's last hydrofoils were a speedy patrol gunboat, the USS *Flagstaff*, built for the U.S. Navy in 1968, and two gun/missile patrol boats, built for the Israeli Navy in the early 1980s. However, these were all really experimental programs and are no longer built by Grumman. Someday, large numbers of hydrofoils may be built; many of them based on the pioneering work of Grumman.

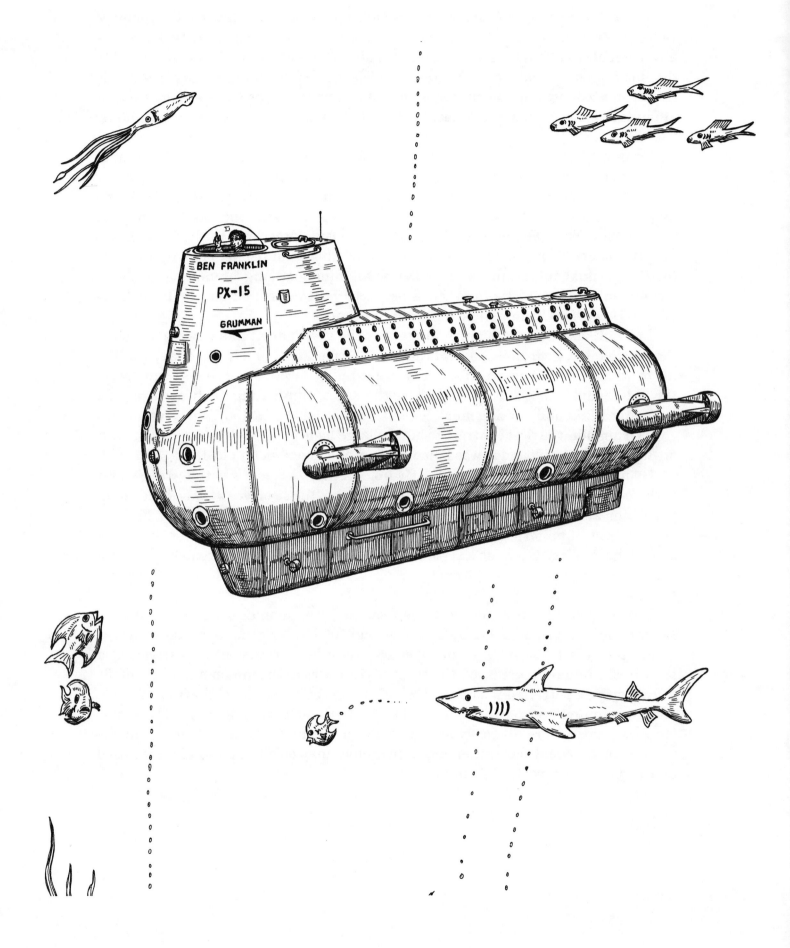

35. Long Island Submarines

Several submarines have been designed and built on Long Island, starting with J. P. Holland's submarine testing station at New Suffolk on the North Fork, between 1899 and 1906. The most famous submarine designed on Long Island came from an aircraft company. When Grumman began its Ocean Systems Group in the 1960s, most aerospace companies had some sort of underwater program. In order to establish a reputation in underwater activity and to provide some practical experience, Grumman formed an alliance with Jacques Piccard, Swiss physicist and underwater researcher.

Piccard was interested in a Gulf Stream Drift Mission in which several men in a submarine would drift along in the Gulf Stream current in the Atlantic Ocean and study it. Grumman designed the PX-15 in Bethpage. This submarine, which was able to go down to 2,000 feet, had plenty of viewing portholes, and a life-support system that could maintain six men for a month. The 130–ton submarine, now named the *Ben Franklin*, was launched at Grumman's facility in Florida, in September 1968.

Piccard and five companions started the drift mission on July 14, 1969, and drifted north with the Gulf Stream Current at depths ranging from 600 to 2,000 feet for 1,500 miles. They surfaced off Nova Scotia thirty days later.

During its successful drift, the *Ben Franklin* collected a great deal of scientific data. Two of its most striking discoveries were that there is relatively little fish life in the Gulf Stream, and that, after passing Cape Hatteras, for some unknown reason, the stream doubles in speed. During the mission, Grumman also carried on physical and mental tests for NASA, comparing submarine life to a long space mission.

Republic Aviation Corporation, in Farmingdale, also designed and built an experimental submarine, the X-1, for the U.S. Navy. It was forty-nine feet long, weighed thirty tons, and could carry a four- or five-man crew. It was tested off Montauk Point in 1964.

36. Maritime Training on Long Island

Future merchant mariners (officers on freighters) and marine engineers (ship designers) have been trained on Long Island from the 1940s to the present. In Glen Cove, the Webb Institute of Naval Architecture teaches future maritime engineers about ship design and construction, so that one day they will be able to design ships of their own for the Navy or merchant fleets.

Webb Institute was founded in 1889, in the Bronx, by shipbuilder William H. Webb. The college moved to Long Island in 1949. It is located on the 26–acre former Herbert L. Pratt estate. The mansion, built in 1912, is now Stevenson Taylor Hall.

Since 1943, the United States Merchant Marine Academy in Kings Point has been training men to be officers in the United States Merchant Marine and leaders of the maritime industry. It is one of five federal academies, similar in operation to West Point and Annapolis, and in 1974 was the first to admit women. The Merchant Marine Academy draws its student body of about 860 from every state and since its founding, it has graduated more than 20,000 shipboard officers.

The Academy's 80–acre campus on the North Shore of Long Island overlooks Long Island Sound and provides a very practical location for maritime training. The Academy is located on a estate formerly owned by Henri Bendel and later Walter P. Chrysler. The federal government purchased the estate in the late 1930s. The mansion is now Wiley Hall, the administration center.

Tuition is free at the United States Merchant Marine Academy and at Webb Institute, which is privately endowed, but admission standards are very high. Students graduate with engineering degrees from these institutions. The United States Merchant Marine Academy is the only one of the service academies which has battle flags because its cadets served in World War II, the Korean Conflict, Vietnam War, and Desert Storm.

Every hour of every day cargo ships of all types sail the waters in and around our nation. They leave our ports full of United States products bound for foreign markets or arrive in our harbors with merchandise and materials for American consumers. There are tankers traveling along the West Coast with oil for our refineries, Great Lakes vessels loaded with iron ore, coal, or other minerals for America's industry, huge container ships in East Coast ports, their box-like containers filled with manufactured goods, general cargo ships in the Gulf of Mexico unloading coffee and fruits, tugboats pushing and pulling barges carrying the Midwest's grain.

These kinds of ships, owned by American companies, make up the United States Merchant Marine. This fleet is a major part of our system of commerce, guaranteeing our access to foreign sources of raw materials and to foreign markets for sale of our goods. In time of war or national emergency, the United States Merchant Marine becomes vital to national security by delivering military supplies overseas to our forces.

The purpose of the United States Merchant Marine Academy at Kings Point is to make sure that people are available to the nation as shipboard officers and as leaders in the marine field. Graduates of Webb Institute design the ships the Merchant Marine sails.

37. Searching the Seas

The EDO company, of College Point, Queens, was founded by Earl D. Osborne in 1925, originally for the manufacture of seaplane floats. After World War II, it broadened its operations to include the development of advanced marine electronics.

In 1947, EDO entered the field of sonar (sound, navigation, and ranging) with the development of a deep-ocean depth sounder. Several thousand of these units have been built for the navies of the world. Sonar units produce sound signals which bounce off the bottom of any submarines or ships in the area. One was used by the USS *Nautilus*, the first submarine to sail *under* the ice at the North Pole.

In the 1960s, EDO developed a variable depth sonar system for use on Navy frigates and destroyers. The fish-shaped electronic device is lowered from the ship on a long cable to where it can more easily detect submarines in the deeper areas of the ocean where enemy submarines might hide. As it is under water, the device is also not affected by rough weather on the surface. EDO has developed about forty different types of sonar systems.

By the early 1970s, EDO had developed the MK-105 helicopter-towed minesweeping "sea sled." This unmanned hydrofoil unit is towed rapidly on a cable by a helicopter. It is used to detect and destroy underwater mines magnetically. As the helicopter tows it, the hydrofoil wings on the "sea sled" raises its hull out of the water. The MK-105 then electronically imitates the magnetic field generated by a ship, causing enemy mines to explode falsely and harmlessly while the operators are safe in the helicopter. The unmanned seaborne unit is built to withstand the force of the explosion. Many of these units have been made. They have cleared mines from Vietnam harbors, the Suez Canal, and, in the early 1990s, the Persian Gulf.

Today, EDO continues to be ocean minded. Several types of advanced electronic equipment, designed and built by EDO, are in operation aboard ships of the United States and foreign navies. This is among the most advanced electronics equipment built on Long Island today.

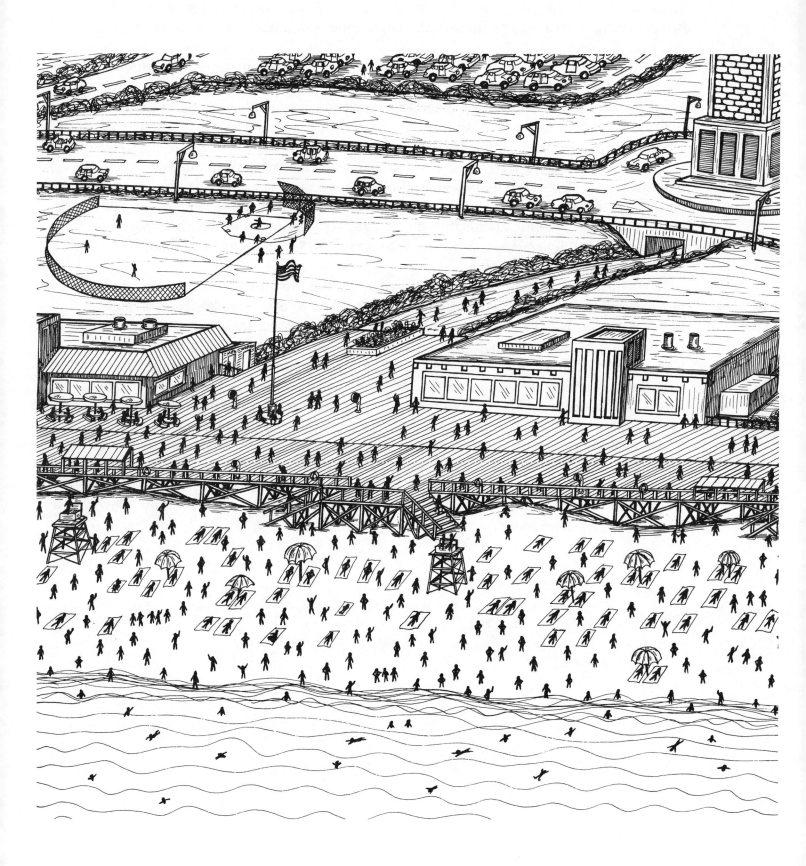

38. The Beaches

With more than 1,000 miles of shoreline, Long Island has many fine beaches. In fact, nearly everyone on Long Island lives within fifteen minutes of a beach. In Nassau and Suffolk Counties alone, there are 160 beaches on the Sound, Peconic Bay, and the ocean side of the South Shore. Geology and geography are the main reasons so many beaches exist on the Island. The endless pounding of the ocean has beaten much of the South Shore into fine sand. Lesser wave action has left North Shore cliffs and rocks intact, but even here erosion has carved out many wonderful beaches.

The beaches on Long Island are managed by a variety of agencies. The federal government oversees the Fire Island National Seashore, while New York State operates seven major beaches. Nassau and Suffolk Counties each administer five beaches, and Long Island's cities, towns, and villages run the rest of the public beaches. The seven state beaches are Orient, Hither Hills, Wildwood, Governor Alfred E. Smith/ Sunken Meadow, Heckscher, Robert Moses, and Jones Beach.

The most popular beach on Long Island is Jones Beach on the South Shore of Nassau County. Since its creation in 1929, Jones Beach has been visited by half a billion people who have enjoyed its facilities, white sand, boardwalk, and wonderful views. Before 1929, Jones Beach was an isolated, swampy sandbar accessible only by small boats and infrequent ferries to a small High Hill Beach. In 1925, the newly formed Long Island State Park Commission, with the strong leadership of Robert Moses, became interested in developing this valuable piece of property. After much political maneuvering and development, on August 4, 1929, Jones Beach State Park opened to the public. Unlike earlier public projects, the buildings at Jones Beach were designed to be light, airy, and attractive. The project itself was built on a scale unlike anything ever seen at a public park in America. Its beach alone was more than six miles long. On the day the park opened, 25,000 cars came, and in its first month of operation, more than 325,000 people visited it. Obviously, there was a tremendous demand for such a park. In 1930, attendance was 1.5 million; by 1932, it had risen to 3.2 million. Jones Beach quickly achieved national prominence. Its high stone water tower, bathhouses, pools, landscaped boardwalk, and adjoining play areas became a model of planned public recreation. Its facilities include a restaurant, cafeteria, bandshell, picnic areas, boat basin, theater, roller rink, miniature golf course, softball fields, and shuffleboard courts as well as paddle tennis courts.

Jones Beach is still one of America's most popular beaches. It now attracts more than 8 million visitors per year. The 2,400–acre park is open all year, but it is most popular during the summer months. Today, Jones Beach is many different things to many different people. Parts of the park appeal to birdwatchers, astronomers, sport fishermen, concert-goers, dancers, surfers, skaters, and golfers, as well as swimmers and sun-bathers. Long Islanders are fortunate to have so many fine public parks and beaches with such wonderful facilities just a few miles away, no matter where we live on the Island.

39. Long Island Waters Today

Boats of all types are still found in great numbers in the waters off Long Island. On Long Island Sound, hundreds of colorful sails of racing fleets may often be seen. However, the racing fleets are only a small part of the maritime scene. Many other boats, large and small, under sail and power, can also be seen criss-crossing the Sound and Great South Bay in every direction. Sailing is still very popular along both shores of the Island, and during the warm months, several major sailboat races are held off its northern and eastern shores. Although slower than powerboats, sailors "riding the wind" experience the same sense of power and exhilaration that carried the earliest humans across the seas.

What has made the waters off Long Island the leading pleasure boating area in the United States? Accessibility is the principal answer, since many millions of people live on Long Island and in New York City. A large number of those millions can afford a boat of some kind, from a rowboat to a sailing yacht. Other advantages of Long Island waters are their geography—protection from the open sea—and their excellent facilities. The many fine harbors and bays are perfect for powerboats or sailboats. It has more than 300 marinas and yacht clubs. Vehicles hauling boat-trailers are a common sight on Long Island roads much of the year. On a nice summer day, Long Island's harbors often resemble a busy airport with boats of all sizes coming, going, and being launched. With more than 1,000 miles of coastline, Long Island is one of the world's major areas for boating and fishing.

Most of the boats regularly seen on the waters off Long Island are for sport and pleasure, but many are still used commercially for fishing and clamming. In fact, fishing, oystering, clamming, and crabbing are important to the economy of the Island. At Montauk alone, fifty world's records for sport fishing have been set in the last ten years. These included a tuna weighing about 800 pounds and a mako shark weighing about 300 pounds. Clearly, with so many harbors and bays, Long Island is a fisherman's paradise. Water temperature and depth vary widely. So do fish species. Some kinds are seasonal, and even when in season, they don't always go to the same spots. However, there are areas where large numbers of fish can usually be caught. Word of locations where fish are biting spreads quickly among Long Island's marinas and fishing stations.

Whether dropping a line from a pier or heading out into the open seas in a big fishing boat, Long Islanders never have to worry about finding fish. At least two dozen edible kinds live in the waters off Long Island throughout the year. Bluefish and mackerel can be found in the Sound. Blackfish, flounder, porgies, striped bass, and weakfish swim in the bays and shorelines along both the North and South Shores. Fluke are often in the Great South Bay, and bluefish and codfish can be found in the water south of Fire Island. Sea bass and pollock often are caught off Long Island's east end, while marlin, tuna and sharks swim in the deep waters east of Montauk.

Fishing shacks, reminders of those used by baymen a century ago, can still be seen along Long Island's South Shore today. These simple wooden "bay houses" are built on low-lying islands or marshes and serve as family fishing and clamming bases during the warm months. Once there were hundreds, but today only a few dozen remain to remind us of a way of life that is rapidly disappearing. Shipbuilding also continues on Long Island, with the biggest shipbuilder being the Menger Boatworks in Bay Shore. Since 1976, Menger has built fifty-five oysterboats, tugboats, and more than a hundred fifteen- to twenty-three-foot-long-"catboats"—a steady, flat-bottomed type of sailboat. At the turn of the century, there were seventy-five catboat builders on Long Island, but today, Menger is the only one left. Long Island-built sailboats can still be seen sailing up and down both coasts of the United States.

Although it is still a major recreational and commercial resource, in recent years Long Island Sound has developed several major problems. Toxic chemicals pollute its harbors; floating garbage washes up on its shores. Millions of gallons of sewage are dumped into it every day, creating high bacteria counts that close its beaches and ban shellfishing. Today the Sound is a waterway that is both thriving and threatened. It still teems with marine life, yet hundreds of fish are killed by pollution every summer. Fortunately, research is now being done on ways to reduce pollution in the Sound, and steps to clean it are underway.

If you want to learn more about our wonderful and exciting maritime heritage, visit one of the many marine museums or historic sites on the Island (see pp. 104-5 below). You can take a ride on the Port Jefferson Ferry and imagine the Golden Age of Steamboating. Ferries from Greenport and Sag Harbor go to Shelter Island, and there are many ferries to Fire Island. You can cruise Long Island Sound on excursion vessels sailing from North Shore ports or go on a commercial fishing party boat from Freeport, Captree, Montauk, or other ports. You can walk along the shore and think of all the ships that have sailed by or perhaps come ashore to land pirates, pick up cargo, or be sheltered from a storm. You can swim or surf and just enjoy maritime Long Island.

To me the sea is a continual miracle,
The fishes that swim—the rocks—the motion of the waves—
   the ships with men in them,
What stranger miracles are there?

Walt Whitman, "Miracles," 1881

A hundred years hence, or ever so many hundred years hence,
   others will see them
Will enjoy the sunset, the pouring-in of the flood-tide
   the falling-back to the sea of the ebb-tide.

Walt Whitman, "Crossing Brooklyn Ferry," 1855

Further Reading for Younger Readers

Long Island

Burchard, Peter. *Whaleboat Raid*. New York: Coward, McCann and Geoghegan, 1977. Historical fiction.

Carse, Robert. *Winter of the Whale, a Novel*. New York: Putnam, 1961. Historical fiction of Indian whaling.

Crump, Irving. *Our Merchant Marine Academy, Kings Point*. New York: Dodd, Mead, 1959.

Farrell, Vivian. *Robert's Tall Friend: A Story of the Fire Island Lighthouse*. Plainview: Island-Metro Publications, Inc., 1987.

Johnson, Harry and Frederick S. Lightfoot. *Maritime New York in Nineteenth-Century Photographs*. New York: Dover, 1980. Includes sections on the Brooklyn Navy Yard, Brooklyn waterfront, and Long Island.

Levy, Mimi Cooper. *Whaleboat Warriors*. New York: Viking, 1963. Historical fiction.

Marhoefer, Barbara. *Witches, Whales, Petticoats, and Sails*. Port Washington: Ira J. Friedman, 1971.

Overton, Jacqueline. *Indian Life on Long Island*. Port Washington: I. J. Friedman, 1963.

General

American Heritage, editors. *The Story of Yankee Whaling*, New York: American Heritage Publishing, 1959.

Beard, John. *Blue Water Views of Old New York, Including Long Island and the Jersey Shore*. Barre, MA: Scrimshaw Press/Barre, 1970.

Carrick, Carol. *Whaling Days*. New York: Clarion, 1993.

Cobblestone. Issues on "Whaling in America," 5, no. 4, April 1984; "The Seafaring Life," April 1988, 8, no. 4; and "America's Lighthouses," January 1981. (Cobblestone Publishing, 28 Main St., Peterborough, NH 03458; 603-924-7209).

Copeland, Peter F. *The Story of Whaling Coloring Book*. New York: Dover, 1986.

DePauw, Linda Grant. *Seafaring Women*. Boston: Houghton Mifflin, 1982.

Fox, Paula. *The Slave Dancer: A Novel*. Scarsdale, NY: Bradbury Press, 1973.

Holling, Holly Clancy. *Seabird*. Boston: Houghton Mifflin, 1948.

Kraus, Scott D. *The Search for the Right Whale*. New York: Crown, 1993.

Latham, Jean Lee. *Carry on, Mr. Bowditch*. Boston: Houghton Mifflin, 1955.

Lauber, Patricia. *Great Whales, the Gentle Giants*. New York: H. Holt, 1991.

Reinfeld, Fred. *The Real Book About Whales and Whaling*. Garden City, NY: Garden City Books, 1960.

This is a sampling; libraries will have other titles.

Bibliography

Bailey, Paul. *Long Island Whalers*. Amityville, NY: Privately printed, 1959.

Bauer, Jack. *A Maritime History of the United States*. Columbia: University of South Carolina Press, 1988.

Beard, John, ed. *Blue Water Views of Old New York*. Barre, MA: Scrimshaw Press, 1970.

Berg, Daniel. *Wreck Valley: A Record of Shipwrecks off Long Island's South Shore*. Lynbrook, NY: Aqua Explorers, 1986.

Blanchard, Fessenden. *Long Island Sound*. Princeton: Van Nostrand, 1958.

Bockstoce, John. *Whales, Ice, and Men*. Seattle: University of Washington Press, 1986.

Botting, Douglas. *The Pirates*. Alexandria, VA: Time-Life, 1978.

Carse, Robert. *Rum Row*. New York: Rinehart, 1959.

Cash, Floris Barnett. "African-American Whalers: Images and Reality," *Long Island Historical Journal* 2 (Fall 1989): 41–52.

Church, Albert. *Whale Ships and Whaling*. New York: W.W. Norton, 1938.

Cole, John N. *Striper: A Story of Fish and Man*. Boston: Atlantic Monthly Press, 1978.

Dow, George Francis. *Whale Ships and Whaling: A Pictorial History*, 1925. Reprint, New York: Dover, 1985.

Dunbaugh, Edwin. *The Era of the Joy Line, 1900-1907*. Westport, CT: Greenwood Press, 1982.

———. *Long Island Sound Steamboats*. Roslyn, NY: Nassau County Museum of Fine Art, 1984.

———. *Night Boat to New England, 1815–1900*. Westport, CT: Greenwood Press, 1992.

———. *A History of Webb Institute*. Forthcoming from Webb Institute.

———. "Webb Institute of Naval Architecture," *Nassau County Historical Society Journal* 58 (1993): 13–20.

Dyson, Verne. *Anecdotes and Events in Long Island History*. Port Washington, NY: Ira Friedman, 1969.

Earle, Walter K. *Scrimshaw: Folk Art of the Whalers*. Cold Spring Harbor: Whaling Museum Society, 1957.

Edwards, Everett. *Whale Off!* New York: Coward-McCann, 1932.

Gabriel, Ralph. *The Evolution of Long Island: A Story of Land and Sea*, 1921. Reprint, Port Washington, NY: Ira Friedman, 1960.

Gonzalez, Ellice B. *Storms, Ships and Surfmen: The Life Savers of Fire Island*. New York: Fire Island National Seashore, 1982.

Hamilton, Harlan. *Lights and Legends: A Historical Guide to the Lighthouses of Long Island Sound*. Stamford, CT: Wescott Cove Publishing, 1987.

Holden, Albert. *A Pictorial History of Montauk*. Montauk, NY: Holden's, 1983.

Johnson, Harry and Frederick S. Lightfoot. *Maritime New York in Nineteenth-Century Photographs*. New York: Dover, 1980.

Johnson, Madeleine. *Fire Island, 1650–1980*. Mountainside, NJ: Shoreland Press, 1983.

Luke, Myron and Robert Venables. *Long Island in the American Revolution*. Albany: New York State Bicentennial Commission, 1976.

MacKay, Anne, ed. *She Went A-Whaling: The Journal of Martha Smith Brewer Brown*. Orient: Oysterponds Historical Society, 1993.

MacKay, Robert, et al. *Between Ocean and Empire*. Northridge, CA: Windsor Publications, 1985.

Malley, Richard C. *In Their Hours of Leisure: Scrimshaw in the Cold Spring Harbor Whaling Museum*. Cold Spring Harbor: Whaling Museum Society, 1993.

Manley, Sean. *Long Island Discovery*. Garden City, NY: Doubleday, 1966.

Marhoefer, Barbara. *Witches, Whales, Petticoats, and Sails*. Port Washington: Kennikat, 1971.

Matthiessen, Peter. *Men's Lives: The Surfmen and Baymen of the South Fork*. New York: Random House, 1986.

McAdams, Roger Williams. *"Salts of the Sound": A Story of Steamboating on Long Island Sound from 1815 to the Present*. Brattleboro, VT: Stephen Day Press, 1939.

Murphy, Robert C. *Fish-Shape Paumanok: Nature and Man on Long Island*, 1964. Reprint, Great Falls, VA: Waterline Books, 1991.

Payne, Robert. *The Island* (Gardiners Island). New York: Harcourt, Brace, 1958.

Rachlis, Eugene. *They Came to Kill: The Story of Eight Nazi Saboteurs in America*. New York: Random House, 1961.

Radcliffe, Lewis. "Long Island Shell Fisheries," *Long Island; A History*, ed. Paul Bailey. 2: 1–16. New York: Lewis Publishing, 1949.

Randel, William Pierce. "'The Flames of Hell Gate': *General Slocum* Disaster." *American Heritage* 30 (Sept./Nov. 1979): 62–75.

Rattray, Jeannette. *Ship Ashore!* Southampton, NY: Yankee Peddler Book Co., 1955.

Reeves, Henry A. "The Commerce, Navigation and Fisheries of Suffolk County," in *Bi-Centennial: A History of Suffolk County*, pp. 55–78. Babylon, 1885; reprint, County of Suffolk, 1983. Appendices have statistical data on fisheries and ship building, pp. 93–125.

Schmitt, Frederick. *Mark Well the Whale!* Cold Spring Harbor, NY: Whaling Museum Society, 1986.

——. *Whale Watch: The Story of Share Whaling Off Nassau County, New York*. Cold Spring Harbor: Whaling Museum Society, 1972. Originally in *Nassau County Historical Society Journal*, "The 'Whaling Designe' of Nassau County," 31 (1971): 30–38.

Shodell, Elly. *Cross Currents: Baymen, Yachtsmen and Long Island Waters, 1830s–1990s*. Port Washington: Port Washington Library, 1993.

Skinner, Alanson. *The Indians of Manhattan Island and Vicinity*. New York: American Museum of Natural History, 1947.

Smits, Edward J. *Nassau: Suburbia, USA*. Garden City, NY: Doubleday, 1974.

Solomon, Nancy with Paul Bentel and Martha Cooper. *On the Bay: Bay Houses and Maritime Culture on Long Island's Marshlands*. Syosset: Friends for Long Island Heritage, 1992.

Stone, Gaynell, ed. *The Shinnecock Indians: A Culture History*. Suffolk County Archaeological Association, Readings in Long Island Archaeology and Ethnohistory, vol. 6. Lexington, MA: Ginn Custom Printing, 1983. See "The Circassian Story: We'll Float Tonight or We'll Go to Hell!" by Carolyn Erland Brower, pp. 367–99.

Taylor, Lawrence. *Dutchmen on the Bay*. Philadelphia: University of Pennsylvania Press, 1983.

Valentine, Harriet G. and Andrus T. *An Island's People: "One Foot in the Sea, One on Shore."* Huntington, NY: Peterson Press, 1976.

Van Popering, Marinus J. and Joseph B. Glancy. "History of the Shellfish Industry," *Long Island Forum* 10 (1947): 163–65, 175–76, 189, 193–94, 207–8, 214.

Weigold, Marilyn. *The American Mediterranean: An Environmental, Economic, and Social History of Long Island Sound*. Port Washington, NY: Kennikat, 1974.

Welch, Richard F. *An Island's Trade: Nineteenth-Century Shipbuilding on Long Island*. Mystic, CT: Mystic Seaport Museum, 1993.

Welles, Gordon. *Port Jefferson*. Port Jefferson: Historical Society of Port Jefferson, 1977.

Williamson, W. H. *Adriaen Block*. New York: Museum of the City of New York, 1959.

Wilson, Rufus. *Historic Long Island*. New York: Berkeley Press, 1902.

Wissler, Clark. *The Indians of Greater New York*. New York: AMS Press, 1975.

Wood, Clarence Ashton. "Bunker Fishing in Peconic Bay," *Long Island Forum* 8 (1945): 183, 197–98, 205, 217–18.

——"Try Pots and Fish Factories," *Long Island Forum* 19 (1956): 23–24, 37, 49, 52.

Long Island Maritime Museums and Related Sites

You should call for hours; some are open only seasonally. Most museums charge a small admission fee or ask for a donation. For additional information, see Raymond Spinzia, Judith Spinzia, and Kathryn Spinzia, *Long Island: A Guide to New York's Suffolk and Nassau Counties*, revised edition (New York: Hippocrene Books, 1991) and SCOPE, *Where to Go and What to Do on Long Island* (New York: Dover, 1993).

American Merchant Marine Museum, U.S. Merchant Marine Academy, Steamboat Rd., Kings Point; (516) 773–5515 or 466–9696.

Boat Shop, East Hampton Historical Society, 42 Gann Rd., East Hampton; (516) 324–6850.

Cold Spring Harbor Whaling Museum, Main St. (Route 25A), Cold Spring Harbor; (516) 367–3418.

Cruises on Long Island Sound or Great South Bay from Glen Cove, Huntington, Greenport, Freeport, Captree, Bay Shore, and Patchogue. See listings in "Events" section, *Newsday,* Part 2 on Fridays.

Custom House, Main and Garden Sts., Sag Harbor; (516) 941–9444.

East End Maritime Museum and *Regina Maris* (Long Island's only tall ship), 1 Bootleg Alley (at Wiggins St.), Greenport; (516) 477–0004.

East Hampton Town Marine Museum, Bluff Rd., Amagansett; (516) 267–6544 or 324–6850. Exhibits on whaling, fishing, and eastern Long Island's marine heritage.

Eatons Neck Coast Guard Station and Lighthouse, Asharokan; (516) 261–6868, Group tours only, by appointment.

Ferries: to Fire Island from Bay Shore, Sayville, and Patchogue; to Bridgeport from Port Jefferson; to New London from Orient Point and Montauk; to Shelter Island from Greenport and Sag Harbor.

Fire Island Coast Guard Station, Robert Moses State Park, Fire Island; (516) 661–9101. Group tours only, by appointment.

Fire Island Lighthouse and Museum, Fire Island National Seashore, east of Robert Moses State Park, parking field 5, Fire Island; (516) 321–7028 or 661–4876.

Horton Point Lighthouse and Marine Museum (off Lighthouse Rd.), Southold; (516) 765–2101 or (516) 765–5500. A working lighthouse and marine museum.

Long Island Aquarium. Two aquariums were proposed in 1993, one in Riverhead under the direction of Okeanos and the other in Bay Shore.

Long Island Maritime Museum, 86 West Ave. (off Montauk Highway), West Sayville; (516) 854–4974. Formerly Suffolk Marine Museum. Large collection of small craft and permanent exhibits on oystering, shipwrecks, and lifesaving.

Long Island Surfing Museum, 50 E. Main St., Babylon; (516) 661–1526.

Marine Nature Study Area, Hempstead Estuary, 500 Slice Drive, Oceanside; (516) 766–1580.

Maritime Center at Norwalk, 10 North Water Street, South Norwalk, CT 06854; (203) 838–1488.

Mather House Museum, 115 Prospect St., Port Jefferson; (516) 473–2665. Shipbuilder's house; ships' artifacts and shipbuilding tools in marine barn.

Montauk Point Lighthouse and Museum, Montauk Point, Montauk; (516) 668–2544.

Mount Sinai Marine Sanctuary Nature Center, Harbor Beach Rd., Mount Sinai; (516) 473–8346 or 654–7914.

Museums at Stony Brook, 1208 Route 25A, Stony Brook, 11790; (516) 751–0066. Permanent exhibit of duck decoys in History Museum; Mount paintings exhibited in Art Museum may feature maritime themes.

Mystic Seaport Museum, Inc., Route 27 (P.O. Box 600), Mystic, CT 06355; (203) 572–0711.

New York Aquarium, Coney Island, Brooklyn; (718) 265–3474.

Northport Historical Museum, 215 Main St., Northport; (516) 757–9859. Permanent shipbuilding exhibit.

Okeanos Ocean Research Foundation, 278 E. Montauk Hwy., P.O. Box 776, Hampton Bays: (516) 728–4522. Whale watch cruises from Montauk; marine education and research.

Phillips House Museum, 28 Hempstead Avenue, Rockville Centre; (516) 766–5706. An 1882 ship captain's house.

Port Washington Pilot House Museum, Port Washington docks.

Sag Harbor Whaling and Historical Museum, Main and Garden Sts., Sag Harbor; (516) 725–0770.

Shinnecock Coast Guard Station, 100 Foster Ave., Hampton Bays; (516) 728–0078.

South Street Seaport Museum, 12 Fulton Street, New York, NY 10038; (212) 669–9400.

Stirling Historical Society, Main and Adams St., Greenport; (516) 477–0099.

Suffolk County Historical Society Museum, 300 W. Main St., Riverhead; (516) 727–2881. Permanent displays of ship models, half-models, and whaling.

United States Merchant Marine Academy, Kings Point; (516) 773–5387.

Vanderbilt Marine Museum, Little Neck Rd., Centerport; (516) 262–7800. Specimens collected by William K. Vanderbilt, Jr.

Marine Education Centers

Alvernia Center for Environmental Studies
Box 301
105 Prospect Road
Centerport, NY 11721
(516) 261-5160

Center of Marine Development
    and Research
Kingsborough Community College
The City University of New York
2001 Oriental Blvd.
Brooklyn, NY 11235
(516) 718-368-5525

Cornell Cooperative Extension of
    Nassau County
Plainview Complex, Building J
1425 Old Country Road
Plainview, NY 11803-5015
(516) 454-0900, Ext. 248

Cornell Cooperative Extension of Suffolk
Marine Program
39 Sound Avenue
Riverhead, NY 11901-5018
(516) 727-3910

Great Neck Outdoor Education Center
Great Neck Public Schools
345 Lakeville Road
Great Neck, NY 11020
(516) 773-1463

Maritime Center on Long Island
Box 991
Huntington, NY 11743
(516) 385-7743

Nassau BOCES Outdoor Education Office
Salisbury Center
Valentines and The Plain Road
Westbury, NY 11590
(516) 997-8700, Ext. 264

Education Department
New York Aquarium
Boardwalk and W. 8th Street
Brooklyn, NY 11224
(516) 718-265-3400

New York Sea Grant
Cornell University Laboratory
39 Sound Avenue
Riverhead, NY 11901-1017
Phone: (516) 727-3910
Fax: (516) 369-5944

New York Sea Grant Extension Program
125 Nassau Hall
SUNY at Stony Brook
Stony Brook, NY 11794-5002
Phone: (516) 632-8730
Fax: (516) 632-8216

Okeanos Ocean Research Foundation, Inc.
278 E. Montauk Hwy., Box 776
Hampton Bays, NY 11948
(516) 728-4522

Queens College Center for Environmental
    Teaching and Research
Caumsett State Park
Huntington, NY 11743
(718) 520-7240
(516) 421-3526

Roosevelt Sanctuary
134 Cove Road
Oyster Bay, NY 11771
(516) 922-3200

SUNY/Stony Brook
Maritime Sciences Research Center
Stony Brook, NY 11794-5002

Suffolk County Marine Environmental
    Learning Center
Cornell Cooperative Extension Marine
    Education Program
39 Sound Avenue
Riverhead, NY 11901-1098
727-3910

Town of Huntington Department of
    Environmental Control
100 Main Street
Huntington, NY 11743
351-3186

U.S. Dept. of the Interior
Fish and Wildlife Service
Box 608
Islip, NY 11751
(516) 581-1538

About the Author and Illustrator

Joshua Stoff is a native Long Islander. He was a history major at Adelphi and received his M.A. in Museum Studies from the University of Toronto. He is Curator of the Cradle of Aviation Museum at Mitchel Field in Garden City.

Mr. Stoff is the author of two other books published by Hofstra University's Long Island Studies Institute, *The Aerospace Heritage of Long Island* (1989) and, for younger readers, *From Airship to Spaceship: Long Island in Aviation and Spaceflight* (1991). The other books he has written and illustrated for young readers are *Dirigible* and *The Voyage of the Ruslan* which is a story about the first manned expedition to Mars. *The Voyage of the Ruslan* has been translated into Russian and reprinted in the Soviet Union.

Mr. Stoff wrote *The Aerospace Heritage of Long Island* (1989), *The Thunder Factory: The History of the Republic Aviation Corporation* (1990), and *A Picture History of World War II American Aircraft Production* (1993) and has co-authored books on *Roosevelt Field World's Premier Airport* (1992) and *Chariots for Apollo: The Making of the Lunar Module* (1985).

Joshua Stoff is married and lives on Long Island with his wife Jill and sons Matthew and Tyler. He enjoys flying a 1945 Piper Cub.

Joshua Stoff and his son, Matthew, outside the Cold Spring Harbor Whaling Museum. The cannon was originally on Cannon Hill on the west side of the harbor. It signaled the arrival of homecoming whaling vessels.

The Long Island Studies Institute

The Long Island Studies Institute at Hofstra University encourages the study of Long Island's history and heritage through its publications, conferences, educational services, and reference collections. The institute was established in 1985, and is a cooperative endeavor of Hofstra University and Nassau County. The Institute collections include the Nassau County Museum collection which had been at Eisenhower Park and Hofstra University's James N. MacLean Nassau County American Legion Memorial collection of New York State History. Both these collections, formerly on the ninth floor of Hofstra's Axinn Library, can now be found with the

The offices and collections of the Long Island Studies Institute are located in this building on Hofstra's West Campus.

Department of Special Collections on the second floor of the Library Services Center on the West Campus. The institute also houses the historical research offices of the Nassau County Historian and the Museum Services Division of the Nassau County Department of Recreation and Parks.

For information on Institute publications, conferences, and collections (including hours open to the public), contact the Long Island Studies Institute, West Campus, 619 Fulton Avenue, Hempstead, New York 11550–4575; (516) 463–6411.

Publications

Heart of the Lakes Publishing:

> *Evoking a Sense of Place*, ed. Joann P. Krieg (1988)
> *Robert Moses: Single-Minded Genius*, ed. Joann P. Krieg (1989)
> *Long Island and Literature*, by Joann P. Krieg (1989)
> *The Aerospace Heritage of Long Island*, by Joshua Stoff (1989)
> *Long Island: The Suburban Experience*, ed. Barbara M. Kelly (1990)
> *From Airship to Spaceship: Long Island in Aviation and Spaceflight,* by Joshua Stoff (1991)
> *The Blessed Isle: Hal B. Fullerton and His Image of Long Island, 1897–1927,* by Charles L. Sachs (1991)
> *Theodore Roosevelt: Many-Sided American*, ed. Natalie A. Naylor, Douglas Brinkley, and John Allen Gable (1992)
> *The Roots and Heritage of Hempstead Town*, ed. Natalie A. Naylor (1994)

Long Island Studies Institute:

> *To Know the Place: Teaching Local History*, ed. Joann P. Krieg (1986)
> *Nassau County Historical Society*, Cumulative Index, 1958–1988, by Jeanne M. Burke (1989)
> *The Calderone Theatres on Long Island: An Introductory Essay and Description of the Calderone Theatre Collection at Hofstra University*, by Miriam Tulin (1991)
> *Exploring African-American History*, ed. Natalie A. Naylor (1991)
> *Vignettes of Hempstead Town, 1643–1800*, by Myron H. Luke (1993)

Greenwood Press:

> *Suburbia Re-examined*, ed. Barbara M. Kelly (1989)

Index

Names of ships are italicized and are alphabetized by the first letter of the first word. British naval vessels are identified by the initials HMS which is an abbreviation for Her (or His) Majesty's Ship; USS indicates a United States Ship. Ships without these initials were owned by individuals or private companies rather than the government.

-A-

Adventure, 19
African Americans, 31, 45. *See also* blacks
agriculture, 49
Amagansett, 4, 83
America, 47
America's Cup race, 47, 69
Arizona, USS, 77
Arundo, 87
Atlantic Basin, 55
Atlantic Ocean, 9, 65, 67, 71, 84, 87, 95, 97

-B-

Babylon, 29
Barren Island, 49
bay houses, 99
Bayles shipyard, 47, 73
baymen, 63
Bay Shore, 63
Bayville, 65
beaches, 7, 97
Bellomont, Lord, 19
Ben Franklin, 91
Bethpage, 91
blacks, 9, 29, 45. *See also* African Americans
Block, Adriaen, 9, 15
Block Island, 15, 29
blubber, 17, 31, 33
Blue Point, 43, 65
boats, 67, 89, 99
Bradish, Joseph, 19
Brewster Buffalos, 85
Brewster, Caleb, 25
Bridgeport and Port Jefferson Steamboat Company, 47, 59, 100
Bristol, 39
British, 23, 25, 29
Brookhaven, 45
Brooklyn, 23, 39, 55, 81
Brooklyn Navy Yard, 4, 55, 71, 77
Brown, Edwin, 33
    Martha Smith Brewer, 33

-C-

canoes, 11, 89
Canarsie (Indians), 15
Captree, 67, 100
Carll, Jesse, shipyard, 45
Cedar Island, 27
Center Moriches, 43
Charlie Hickman, 43
Circassian, 43
Civil War, 45, 47, 51, 57
clams, *see* shell fish
Clapham, Thomas, 67
coastal trade, *see* shipping trade
Coast Guard, U.S., 41, 75, 79, 83
Coimbra, 87
Cold Spring Harbor, 4, 35, 37, 45
Cold Spring Harbor Whaling Museum, 31, 45
Concer, Pyrrhus, 31
Coney Island, 15, 63
Connetquot, 11
Continental Iron Works, 57
Cooper, Mercator, 33
Cullen, John C., 83
Culloden, HMS, 23
Currier, Nathaniel, 39–41

-D-

Daisy, 45
Davis, Gil, 63
Debs Inlet, 87
Denison, H.S., 89
Dermer, Thomas, 15
Dolphin, 89
Doxsee family, 65
Drowned Meadow, 47. *See also* Port Jefferson
Dutch, 15, 39
Dutch West India Company, 15

-E-

Eastern Steamship and Colonial Lines, 61
East Hampton, 21, 23, 79
East Rockaway, 53, 87
Eatons Neck, 27, 39

EDO, 95
Edward L. Frost, 47
England, 19, 29
English, 15, 17, 19. *See also* British.
Ericsson, John, 57
Essex, Jr., USS, 29

-F-

Fall River Line, 59, 61
Farmingdale, 91
Farragut, Admiral, 47
Far Rockaway, 39, 81
ferries, 100. *See also* Bridgeport and
        Port Jefferson Steamboat Com-
        pany.
fertilizer, 49
Fire Island, 4, 27, 39, 41, 63, 75, 79, 87,
        100
Fire Island Inlet, 29, 75, 79
Fire Island National Seashore, 97
fishing, 15, 49, 67, 99. *See also* menhaden
fishermen, 67, 99
Fishers Island, 81
Flagstaff, USS, 89
Flower family, 65
Flushing, 59
Fort Hero, 81
Fort Nonsense, 29
forts, 29, 81
Fort St. George, 25
Freeport, 4, 67, 100
Fulton, 55

-G-

Gardiner, John, 19
Gardiner, John Lion, 29
Gardiners Bay, 12, 23, 29
Gardiners Island, 4, 19, 29, 63
General Slocum, 41
Glen Cove, 59, 93
Gould, Howard, 69
Great Eastern, 41
Great Gull Island, 81
Great Neck, 59
Great South Bay, 4, 9, 29, 49, 63, 65, 67,
        99
Great Western, 41
Greenpoint, 57
Greenport, 4, 35, 37, 45, 49, 59, 67, 69,
        79, 87, 100
Grumman, 89, 91
Gull Islands, 27, 81
gyroscopes, 71

-H-

Hempstead Harbor, 59, 63
Henry James, 47
Hercules, 54–55
Hither Hills State Park, 97
Holland, J. P., 99
Hortons Point, 27
Howe, Sir William, 23
Hudson, Henry, 15
Huntington, 27, 45
Huntington Harbor, 63
Huntington Harbor Lighthouse, 27
Huntington Militia, 31
hydrofoil, 89

-I-

Indians, 9, 11–13, 17, 31, 49
island, Long Island as, 7, 9, 15
Islip, 69

-J-

Jamaica Bay, 49
Jamesport, 37
John Milton, 41
Johnson, W. R., 71
Jones Beach, 17, 65, 97
Jones, John H., 37
Jones, Walter R., 37
Juet, Robert, 15

-K-

Kidd, Capt. William, 19
Kings Point, 4, 93

-L-

Lake, 73
Lake Success, 71
Lexington, 39–40
L'Hommedieu, Ezra, 49
Lido Beach, 83
lifesavers, 43
Life-Saving Service, 43
lighthouses, 27
Lloyd Harbor lighthouse, 27
Lloyds Neck, 4, 25, 59
Long Beach, 53, 65
Long Island Railroad, 47, 59, 61, 63, 83
Long Island Sound, 9, 15, 23, 25, 27, 29,
        41, 45, 59, 61, 93, 97, 99–100
Long Island State Park Commission, 97
Long Island Studies Institute, 7, 110
Long Island, USS, 85
Lucy Ann, 33.

-M-

Maine, USS, 77

Manhasset, 11
Manhattan, 31, 33
Manhattan Island, 15, 23. *See also* New
    York City
Margaretha, 43
maritime training, 93
Martha Wallace, 73
Massapequa, 11
Mastic, 25
Mecox, 43
Meigs, Jonathan, 25
menhaden (or mossbunkers), 11, 15, 49-
    51; *see also* fishing
menhaden factories, 49-51
Merchant Marine Academy, U.S., 93
Merrick, 11
Merrimack, 57
Mexico, 39
Missouri, USS, 77
Monitor, 56-57
Montauk (Indians), 13
Montauk (location), 11, 23, 39, 51, 67,
    87, 100
Montauk Point, 4, 7, 9, 15, 27, 41, 75, 81,
    87, 91
Montauk Steamboat Company, 61
Morgan, Governor, 63.
Moriches Bay, 65
Moriches Inlet, 63
Moses, Robert, 97
Moses, Robert, State Park, 97
Mount Sinai, 25
mossbunkers, *see* menhaden
Murphy, Robert Cushman, 45
museums, 7, 100, 106-7

-N-

Nantucket sleigh ride, 31
Nassau, 59
Native Americans, *see* Indians
Nautilus, 95
Navy, 71, 73, 75, 77, 85, 89, 91, 93
Nazi agents, 83
Near Rockaway, 39
New Suffolk, 37, 91
New York (City), 47, 53, 59, 61, 67, 81
New York, USS, 77
Niagara, 55
Noress, 87
Northern Pacific, USS, 75
Northport, 4, 27, 45

-O-

Ockers, Jacob, 65

Ogden, John, 17
Ohio, 55
Old Field, 27
Orient Point, 61, 81
Orient Beach State Park, 97
Oyster Bay, 4, 21, 63, 65, 69, 89
oysters, *see* shellfish

-P-

Park City, 73
Parsons, Samuel, 25
Patchogue, 11, 63
Pearl Harbor, 77
Peconic, 9
Peconic Bay, 11, 45, 49, 97
Pentland, HMS, 87
Perry, Matthew, 33, 47
Piccard, Jacques, 91
Picket Patrol, 87
pirates, 19, 63
Plum Island, 27, 81
Point Lookout, 65
pollution, 100
Poquott, 29
Porter, David, 29
Port Jefferson, 4, 29, 45, 47, 53, 59, 73
Port Jefferson ferry, *see* Bridgeport and
    Port Jefferson Steamboat Com-
    pany
prohibition, 79
Promised Land, 51

-Q-

quahog, *see* shellfish
Quogue, 87

-R-

races, boat, 69, 99
Republic Aviation Corporation, 91
Resor, 87
Revolutionary War, 21, 23, 25
Richards, Daniel, 55
Rockaway, 4, 17, 39, 53, 63, 65
Rockville Centre, 53
Roslyn, 59, 67
Roslyn yawl, 67
Royal Oak, HMS, 23
Roys, Thomas, 35, 37
rumrunning, 79

-S-

sabateurs, 83
Sag Harbor, 4, 29, 35, 100
Sag Harbor Whaling Museum, 31
San Antoinio, 19

San Diego, USS, 75
Savannah, 39
Sayville, 41, 49, 63
scallops, *see* shellfish
Scotia, 43
Sea Cliff, 59
Seawanhaka, 59
Seawanhaka Corinthian Yacht Club, 69
Setauket, 4, 25, 45
Sheepshead Bay, 67
Sheffield, 37
shellfish, 11, 15, 63-65, 99
Shelter Island, 65
Shinnecock, 61
Shinnecock (Indians), 13, 43
Shinnecock Inlet, 27
shipping trade, 9, 15, 21,25, 27, 43, 45, 47, 53, 93
shipbuilding, 9, 21, 45, 47, 53, 67, 73, 99-100
shipwrecks, 23, 39-41, 43
Slocum, see *General Slocum*
Smith, Gov. Alfred E. Smith/Sunken Meadow State Park, 97
Smith Point, 43
Smithtown, 63
sonar system, 95
Southampton, 17, 29
Southold, 21, 27, 49
Spanish-American War, 77, 81
spermaceti, 17
Sperry, Elmer, 71
Sperry Gyroscope Company, 71
Splendid, 37
steamships, 47, 59-61
Stony Brook, 45, 53, 55
Strong, Anna (or Nancy), 25
Strongs Neck, 25
submarines, 75, 83, 87, 91
Sunken Meadow State Park, 97

Supreme Court, U.S., 7
Sylph, HMS, 29

-T-
Tallmadge, Benjamin, 25
Tolten, 87
Townsend, Samuel, 21
trade, *see* shipping trade
try-pots, 17, 31
Turner, USS, 87

-U-
U-boats, *see* submarines
Unisys, 71
U.S. Merchant Marine Academy, 93

-V-
Vanderbilt, William K., Jr., 69
Verrazano Narrows, 81

-W-
wampum, 11, 12
Wanderer, 45
War of 1812, 29
Washington, George, 23, 25, 27
Webb Institute of Naval Architecture, 93
whaleboats, 29, 31, 45
whaleboat raids, 25
whaling, 7, 11, 13, 17, 31-37, 45
whales, 12, 17, 34-35
Whitman, Walt, 7-8, 100
Wildwood State Park, 97
Willets Point, 81
Wilson, Rueben, 47
World War I, 73, 75, 77, 81
World War II, 61, 77, 81, 83, 85, 87, 93
wrecks, *see* shipwrecks

-Y-
yachting, 69, 99

-Z-
Zoroya, 73